# Rendering the Visual Field

# Rendering the Visual Field

## Illusion Becomes Reality

**Kevin Forseth**

VAN NOSTRAND REINHOLD
————————————New York

Library of Congress Catalog Card Number 90-48600
ISBN 0-442-20042-0

*For Katie*

Van Nostrand Reinhold
115 Fifth Avenue
New York, New York 10003

Chapman and Hall
2-6 Boundary Row
London, SE1 8HN, England

Thomas Nelson Australia
102 Dodds Street
South Melbourne 3205
Victoria, Australia

Nelson Canada
1120 Birchmount Road
Scarborough, Ontario MIK 5G4, Canada

16 15 14 13 12 11 10 9 8 7 6 5 4 3 2 1

**Library of Congress Cataloging-in-Publication Data**

Forseth, Kevin.
    Rendering the visual field : illusion becomes reality / Kevin
Forseth.
        p.    cm.
    Includes bibliographical references and index.
    ISBN 0-442-20042-0
    1. Architectural rendering.   I. Title.
NA2780.F67   1991
720'.28'4—dc20                          90-48600
                                    CIP

# Contents

# Preface

This book is written for people interested in, but with little knowledge of, architectural pencil rendering.

The primary goal of this book is to describe strategies and techniques for achieving natural realism in architectural pencil renderings. Because so many of the illustrations in the book depict buildings, a word or two on perpsective constructions is in order here. The text describes black-and-white pencil rendering techniques only. It does not discuss methods of perspective construction. A background in architectural perspective drawing is therefore recommended, particularly for the last chapter of the book.

Each of the 137 carefully illustrated pencil drawings in *Rendering the Visual Field* is a visual example of the kind of rendered realism advocated in the text. To achieve this level of realism, the text encourages the reader to study not just isolated buildings, but entire visual fields, even to the point of tracing photographs.

Clearly, a building cannot be separated from its natural environment, yet that is just what people who are learning to render buildings tend to do. Inexperienced architectural delineators often portray the building well enough, but seldom do they capture the rendering's overall near and far, large and small scale features realistically. To address this problem, the text again emphasizes the importance of drawing the features that surround buildings. This understanding is reiterated throughout the book.

The text divides the pencil rendering process into three stages. In the first stage, the aspiring renderer is encouraged to study existing settings through the unorthodox method of tracing or copying from photographs. In the second phase, the renderer is urged to develop the ability to translate features in photographs into three-dimensional models. In the third and final phase, the renderer is encouraged to bring idea and the reality together into one believeable picture. The book's final chapter includes examples of modestly scaled renderings. These scenes were fashioned from photographic and computer perspective imagery.

The text is further divided into six parts: Pencil equipment and usage; rendering trees and other landscape elements; copying or tracing from photographs; Modelling the illusion; Pictorial effects; Pencil renderings from computer-generated imagery.

## Acknowledgments

More often than not, formidable tasks are completed through the efforts of not one, but many persons. Over the years, this book was nudged along by several talented, patient students. Special thanks to Wade Weisman, Dan Stube, Lee Meyer, and Steve Jamrose. Don Aehl, a superb sketch artist and architectural delineator, deserves specific recognition for his many wonderful rendering contributions.

The three editors who so kindly put up with the years of delay, Wendy Lockner, Everet Smethurst, and Cindy Zigmund, have my gratitude. My brother, Mark, was helpful in writing and editing much of the text. Tim McGinty provided useful criticism of early versions of the manuscript. My wife, Katie, provided many of the preliminary photographs for the book.

## Rendering Credits

The following students contributed renderings to the book:

Figure 1–1. Don Aehl

Figure 1–6. Don Aehl

Figure 1–7. Don Aehl

Figure 1–8. Don Aehl

Figure 1–9. Don Aehl

Figure 2–1. Don Aehl

Figure 3–2. Don Aehl

Figure 3–3. Jeff Weber

Figure 3–4. Jeff Weber

Figure 3–5. Don Aehl

Figure 3–6. Don Aehl

Figure 3–9. Jeremy Greene

Figure 3–10. Angela Shultz

Figure 3–13. Steve Jamrose

Figure 3–14. Dan Stube

Figure 4–9. Wade Weisman

Figure 4–10. Wade Weisman, Paul Knudson, Rene Kubish

Figure 5–1. Don Aehl

Figure 5–3. Don Aehl

Figure 5–5. Don Aehl

Figure 5–7. Don Aehl

Figure 7–2. Joseph Lopera

Figure 7–4. Michael McGann

Figure 7–6. Tate Boho

Figure 7–7. Jung-In Kim

Figure 7–10. Patrick Griffin

Figure 8–2. Mike Zuelhke

Figure 8–6. Jung-In Kim

Figure 8–12. Eric Villarreal

Figure 8–13. Jody Ryg

# Introduction

*If you wish to acquire a good style for mountains, and to have them look natural, take some large stones, sharp-edged and not smooth, and copy them from nature . . .*

CENNINO CENNINI

*Standing on the bare ground—my head bathed by the blithe air and uplifted into infinite space—all mean egoism vanishes. I become a transparent eyeball; I am nothing; I see all.*

RALPH WALDO EMERSON

*You come to nature with your theories, and she knocks them all flat.*

PIERRE AUGUSTE RENOIR

This book was written for the benefit of those who love subtle and precise pencil renderings but have no idea how to draw them. It is about rendered realism.

What exactly is this realism, insofar as it has to do with drawing? Rendered realism portrays subject matter precisely as it appears to the eye.

Moreover, if this realism is lifelike, it drenches the eye with visual imagery so specific it persuades the mind to empathize with the depicted scene. Realism of this sort makes a nearly total claim upon the viewer's senses. It virtually enforces involvement in the depicted scene by triggering the classic "suspension of disbelief" that is so important to drama.

In every setting, urban or rural, in every neighborhood and backyard, we are saturated in realism's abundant potential subject matter. A glance through the book's illustrations attests to this. Many of the book's renderings, notably the landscape portraits of historic places, are set pieces, sumptuous and formal. In other renderings, the scene is "slice of life," capturing candid-camera snapshots of the unexpected in the back alleys of everyday life.

Needless to say, total realism, or in the least some facsimile thereof, is by no means easy to achieve. In practice, the illustrator is confronted with a whole series of behind-the-scenes dilemmas that, in effect, continually demolish attempts to pinpoint its definition. It seems the literal realism of objects at the intimate scale of moth-eaten furniture and nostril hair is not related to the realism of the clear darkness of a late evening sky and beyond.

By convention, the renderer's interpretation of what constitutes realism is rooted in the basic idea that every drawing stands for something that exists on the other side of a transparent picture plane. That is, the rendering is envisioned as a "window" with a view, and something real exists beyond the "picture" in the pane. If the rendering could be opened like the sash of a window, all the smells and climates of the depicted scene might tease the senses. However, and this is important, as the depicted scene extends deeper into the expanding background of pictorial space, the renderer discovers that features in the scene fuse together at an alarming rate. Twigs and branches in the foreground become trees in the midground and woods in the background. Still further into the pictorial distance, the momentum of this ongoing fusion culminates with the seemingly far-fetched, self-conscious realization that the only reality of the rendering process is the opaque surface of the rendering itself. That is to say, with increasing pictorial depth of field, the "let me see life through the picture plane" attitude of basic realism dissolves by stages into an attitude that renderings are themselves objects meant to be looked at and admired on their own terms.

The agent that effects this radical change in interpretation is none other than common sense. It is common sense, for example, that awakens the illustrator to the inescapable conclusion that rendering realistically involves more than just drawing with an eye for detail. The neophyte realist clings to a notion that experienced renderers consider a myth: the idea that the illustrator striving for realism ought to depict every needle on a pine tree in the same way that a child counts marbles—1,2,3 . . . 499,999,998, 499,999,999, 500,000,000. The actual pictorial space is too large, too fluid, and too diverse to render that way.

Common sense also persuades the artist to accept the idea that realism involves depicting things as they appear in context. We live in what ecologists consider an impressive variety of habitats. In light of this abundance of contextural diversity, an object such as a building by itself is not necessarily all that realistic, whereas an object within a believable setting may bring tears to the observer's eyes. In order to gain a foothold on this basic, contextural realism, the text assumes straightaway that the photograph guarantees fidelity to the naked truth of life. The photograph is therefore deemed the perfect medium for learning to draw contexturally. This book therefore advocates the direct copying and tracing of photographic imagery. It is believed that the careful analysis of photographs of places visited is the most effective way to gain deeper insight into rendered realism. In principle, the renderer ought to be able to copy more than the photograph reveals.

## About the Book

On first sight, this book is an instructional manual, a collection of recipes on the pencil rendering process that just happens to lavish as much care and attention upon the vivid depiction of the kneaded eraser as it does upon the portrayal of a 17th-century French garden prospect. As an instruction manual, the book's early chapters discuss the basics of pencil rendering. The text focuses on the familiar "how to" aspects of the drawing process. Chapters on how to sharpen a pencil, how to draw a tree, even how to draw a site plan are included.

The chapters entitled *Magnified Contexts* and *Unfolding Landscapes* challenge the reader to study what exists as it looks to the eye. Through the unorthodox technique of tracing or copying from photographs, the effects of change in scale on rendered realism are brought to light. Two scale progressions are discussed. *Unfolding Landscapes* examines scale progression from the standpoint of the idealism that fueled the step-by-step development of the Italian, French and English Renaissance garden. *Magnified Contexts*, on the other hand, looks at scale progression from a different point of view. Emphasis is on the capturing of subtle, precise and modest realism through the medium of very ordinary, occasionally domestic, settings.

It is one thing to trace pictures, it is yet another to render compelling scenes of places that exist only in our imaginations. The chapter entitled *The Illusion Becomes Real* lays out the main features of the renderer's total visual field. This pivotal chapter literally sets the stage for the difficult problem of constructing predictive renderings. To anybody even vaguely familiar with the drawing process, it is evident that the means of rendering a place that doesn't yet exist is complicated by the fact that opposites coexist in the same pictorial scene. Somewhat rephrased, the architectural rendering process, in that it is predictive, must bring together things that exist and things that are proposed. Photographs capture what exists. Computer imagery captures what is proposed. In that regard, this chapter describes a physical stage upon which the photographic image and the computer construction may come together. The two technologies of photography and computer-aided design have absolutely nothing in common with each other, but relationships and transitions between the two do exist and can be visualized in terms of one overall pictorial field.

The chapter on *The Gentle Art of Persuading the Viewer* acknowledges the fact that the making of an illusion, which is really what a rendering is all about, is difficult to describe in an honest way. In rendering we are always justified in asking ourselves the question "wherein lies the truth of the picture?" Diagramming is advocated as a means of dissecting the many layers of visual meaning that compete for the viewer's attention.

The book's final chapter includes a few example of time-removed drawings of buildings and environments that do not yet exist. Here, in a final synthesis, the pencil rendering process brings the context photo and the computer-aided design together into a single, unique, realistic image.

## The Illusion is Real

The final, culminating, privately pleasurable experience in the rendering process is reached at that magical moment when we get to step back from our work, take in the whole of its technique and composition, and look into its pictorial space. When everything is in balance, when everything is worked out just right, we are projected into a different time and place. The rendering evokes a sensation as real as a view through our own kitchen window.

There is no reason why drawings copied from photographs may not be more realistic than the copied photographs (Figure 1). In 1853 Eugène Delacroix wrote, "Consider such an interesting subject as the scene taking place around the bed of a dying woman, for example; seize and render that ensemble by photography, if that is possible: it will be falsified in a thousand ways. The reason is that, according to the degree of your imagination, the subject will appear to you more or less beautiful, you will be more or less the poet in that scene in which you are an actor; you see only what is interesting, whereas the instrument puts in everything."

*View looking toward the Pantheon in Stourhead Garden, Wiltshire, England.*

# Chapter 1

# The First Simple Pleasure of Rendering: Selecting Equipment

*I love the tools made for mechanics. I stop at the windows of hardware stores. If I could only find an excuse to buy many more of them than I have already bought on the mere pretense that I might have use for them!*

ROBERT HENRI

*The artist needs but a roof, a crust of bread, and his easel, and all the rest God gives him in abundance.*

ALBERT PINKHAM RYDER

*What a subject! The commonness and the uselessness of the thought are abominable; and if only his idea, common and useless at it is, were clear! What are those two figures doing? She makes a gesture which expresses nothing, and another woman, whom one may suppose to be her maid, is seated on the ground, taking off her shoes and stockings.*

EUGÈNE DELACROIX

To the left of my drawing board stand two Medaglia d'Oro coffee cans. Each is stocked with the basic tool of my trade, the wooden pencil. I take one in hand. Its barrel is slim and smooth; its cedar taper, elegant and precise; its graphite tip, the point from which lines are formed. The joy in using a wooden pencil begins with its feel between thumb and middle finger. Is the diameter of the barrel comfortable? Is the pencil too short? When must the stub-end be tossed into the wastebasket?

Equal in importance to the writing instrument is the drawing paper. How well does the paper accept pencil lead? How does the texture of the paper feel under the even pressure of graphite over its surface? Is the paper gritty, like sandpaper? Is it smooth, like glass?

Further satisfaction will be derived from a good eraser, one that eradicates pencil marks without destroying the tooth of the paper. An eraser that's done its job well reverses time as quickly as the crumbs are brushed away.

Even in the simple act of sharpening a pencil, the smell of fresh cedar and graphite shavings from the wooden pencil's taper evokes memories of grade school and blue-lined tablet paper smelling of pink rubber. The equipment we use most often is denied the critical attention or understanding it deserves. The computer, for all of its unique, heroic qualities, is cold and distant. Pencils are warm. For all of their everyday invisibility, we can grasp them. We can feel them in our hand.

# Color Pencils

The allure of the discount, cut-rate, bargain basement pencil should be resisted at all costs. The supermarket variety of color pencil is not a suitable rendering instrument. Its lead, the consistency of baked clay, does not adhere to paper. Not until enough pencil pressure is applied to destroy the tooth of the paper does the color of the lead begin to appear.

Other pencils to avoid include those that claim to perform a variety of tasks. Water color pencils, for example, should be regarded with suspicion. In their dry state, they function adequately. As a water color medium, they are in a league all of their own, best left to the artistic alchemist for experimentation.

The illustrations for this book were rendered with the Berol Prismacolor Black no. 935. A few were done with the Bruynzeel *design* Black no. 510 (Figure 1–1). The decision to use these black color pencils was based solely on their ability to lay down lines in a full range of tones from black to white.

Color pencils are manufactured in either wax-based or clay-based compositions, neither of which is perfect for every application. Unlike wax pencils, clay pencils don't develop waxy buildup, known as "waxy bloom," a white, filmy layer that may appear days after a color has been applied to a surface. Clay is easier to erase, and likewise smudge, than wax, but its application is harder to control. Clay has one grade of lead hardness and thickness, whereas wax may vary in both of these categories. Wax pencils create a slight shine under certain lighting conditions; clay renderings are without luster whatever the lighting angle. Wax pencils are generally more available than, and compare in cost with, clay pencils.

Berol makes two wax-based pencils, one called Prismacolor and the other Verithin. The colors and color names of both products are derived from painters' colors, using organic, nonmodular color designations with names such as Burnt Umber and Yellow Ochre. Prismacolor art pencils have a thick, soft lead that is effective for general, all-purpose applications. Prismacolor Art Stix, cousins to the Prismacolor pencil, have a wide, naked lead useful for broad, heavy applications.

The Verithin art pencil, with its thinner, harder lead, is useful for fine lines and detail applications. Verithins are also effective in touching up Prismacolor renderings because most of the Verithin colors correspond to the Prismacolor designations. In this latter application, variations in batch color are rarely a concern.

Faber-Castell's Spectracolor pencils are another wax based coloring pencil. The color names and actual colors correspond identically to many of the Berol line of pencils, as if both Faber-Castell and Berol were manufactured in the same place. Spectracolor pencils are, in many respects, identical to Berol's Prismacolor pencils.

Cumberland Derwent pencils are also wax-based. In addition to the usual range of vivid, pure colors, Cumberland Derwents include a selection of pastel colors. A plus for landscape rendering, Derwent offers a wider range of greens than either the Berol or Faber-Castell brands.

Bruynzeel manufactures clay-based pencils that exhibit a "chalky" quality in their application. The color range is broad and vivid.

My choice for best overall pencil remains the Berol Prismacolor Black. It delivers smooth and consistent tones ranging from deepest black to nearly white. Aside from the occasional pencil with brittle lead or the pencil with the loose lead in the wooden barrel, it has performed well over the years.

**Figure 1–1.** *A Berol Prismacolor 24 pencil set is illustrated left, a Bruynzeel pencil set is shown far right.*

## Graphite Pencils

Graphite is applied to paper using one of three types of pencil instruments (Figure 1–2). The simplest, most basic type is the common wooden lead pencil, the kind that fits comfortably behind a carpenter's ear, kept sharp with either an electric sharpener, hand-held sharpener, or knife. The second type of graphite pencil instrument is the traditional lead-holder pencil, often used by architectural draftspersons, a mechanical pencil that requires both manual lead feed control and manual sharpening. The third type, the automatic-feed mechanical pencil, utilizes .3, .5, .7, or .9 mm leads that do not require sharpening. The half-millimeter lead variety is most commonly used.

The auto-feed pencil is generally regarded as superior to the other two types. Its lead remains a constant .5 millimeter in length as it is fed through the pencil's metal sleeve, thereby eliminating the need for sharpening. This is a great time-saving advantage. It also ensures greater consistency of lineweight throughout a drawing, as is evidenced in the illustrations for books like Francis D.K. Ching's *Architectural Graphics*. Unfortunately, despite the auto-feed graphite pencil's advantages, due to the nature of graphite as a medium, it is not capable of producing the black tone quality found in either wax- or clay-based leads.

## Graphite Lead Designations

Graphite pencils are defined in terms of lead weights that correspond to 17 degrees of hardness. These categories vary from 9H, the hardest and lightest lead, to 6B, the softest and darkest. There is another graphite lead that is useful for rendering purposes and that does not fit into these categories, called Ebony. The lead from an Ebony pencil is somewhat blacker and more dense than equivalently graded graphite leads.

For rendering purposes, F, H, HB, and B represent a good range of medium-hard pencil leads. Good rendering leads in the softer, blacker end of the hardness scale include B, 2B, and 3B leads.

Lead grades ranging from 9H to 2H are not only too hard, but also too gray for the purposes of sketching and rendering. On the other hand, 4B, 5B, and 6B leads are too soft; they break easily, require frequent sharpening, and smudge almost without provocation.

It is difficult to pinpoint a superior graphite lead for rendering and sketching because paper type and drawing surface play such an important role. For instance, some paper stock has a rough tooth, analogous to sandpaper, which grabs the pencil lead and chews it up as fast as it is applied. On the other hand, some paper stock has virtually no tooth to it at all.

Another subtle variable that affects line quality is the drawing surface.

**Figure 1–2.** *Graphite is applied to paper using one of three types of pencil instruments. From left to right, two pencils with lead advancing mechanisms, two mechanical pencils, and two auto-feed pencils.*

The same paper stock will pick up lead differently depending on if it is backed by a hard surface, such as glass, or a soft surface, like cardboard.

In the end, so many factors affect the quality and feel of a drawing that individuals are encouraged to find paper, drawing surface, and lead qualities that suit their particular needs. When I work with graphite, I enjoy using a .5 mm auto-feed pencil containing "B" lead. I apply the lead to ordinary photocopy paper laid out on a Borco (drafting table) surface.

## Pencil Sharpeners

Cheap, disposable sharpeners worth less than a pack of gum often have the effect of discouraging us from pointing our pencils. As their blades lose the capacity to shave away the pencil's wood in crisp ribbons, we begin to avoid using them, and our linework deteriorates.

There are many different types of sharpeners. The most primitive is the pocket knife, which is not technically a sharpener at all. A longtime favorite of the artist, the pocket knife whittles a pencil point to the level of skill of its user. The least expensive instrument designed specifically for the purpose of honing pencil points is the simple, hand-held sharpener, available in many forms. With the hand-held sharpener, the pencil is inserted into a cone-shaped orifice and then rotated against a single sharp blade. Some are basic sharpeners with two or three different sized openings for different diameter pencils. Some include a plastic unit that contains the pencil turnings. Hand-held sharpeners are available in variety of shapes and sizes, ranging from biplanes to lamp posts.

Next in line is the pencil sharpener with a hand crank, the type of sharpener that is usually mounted to a wall. These sharpeners are inexpensive and effective, but they do have a drawback. It is often difficult to mount them within arm's reach of drafting tables.

Conventional, hand-operated pencil sharpeners are sufficient for the armchair artist, but the serious delineator may want to consider buying an electric pencil sharpener. The best pencil sharpeners are the electrics, especially the plug-ins with an auto-stop feature that prevents the pencil from grounding itself down once it has been pointed. I have two of these electric pencil sharpeners on my desk at all times. Battery-operated electrics are portable and sharpen effectively, but their batteries must be recharged or replaced. Electrics that consist of single-blade sharpeners mounted on a shaft that rotates are not recommended.

## Other Rendering Supplies

Over the years, I have accumulated cardboard boxes full of surplus rendering supplies (Figure 1–3). In addition to the usual assortment of rubber bands and paper clips, these boxes contain dozens of dried-out technical felt-tip and fountain pens, electric eraser billet fragments, smudge sticks, and odd bits of pastels.

In my office I also have a drawer near my drafting table that is filled with the equipment that I use most frequently. It contains a brush, which is useful for sweeping away the crumbs that accumulate on the page after making an erasure. There is an erasing shield, beneficial for masking tones in order to create straight lines with an eraser. There are three kinds of eraser: a kneaded rubber eraser, for lightening up or highlighting certain tonal areas; a green eraser, for general-purpose erasing chores; and an eraser stick, looking something like a pencil, which I use to completely erase small rendering mistakes.

The drawer includes masking tape and drafting dots. The masking tape was purchased at a hardware store. It is not drafting tape, which is less sticky than masking tape, and therefore prone to curl up under my parallel ruler. The drafting dots are a favorite of mine. As the name implies, drafting dots are round-shaped pieces of tape fastened to a plastic or wax paper strip. Unlike masking tape, drafting dots have no corners to curl up when running a ruler or straight edge over them. I like them because they are very sticky, and they offer the least resistance to corner curl.

There is a smudge stick. The typical smudge stick is a pencil-shaped device composed of tightly rolled paper. It is used to deliberately smear pencil applications for certain visual effects.

There are two scale rulers in the drawer. One is an architectural ruler, the other an engineer's ruler. The architectural ruler is useful for rendering building plans and elevations; the engineer's ruler for rendering larger scale site plans. There is a twelve-inch variable triangle which can be adjusted to any desired angle.

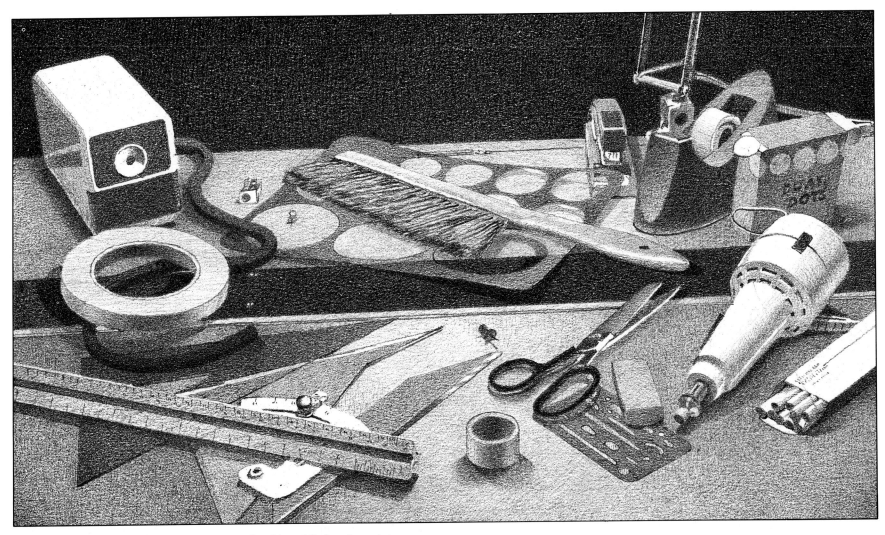

**Figure 1–3.**    *Over the years, I have accumulated cardboard boxes full of surplus rendering supplies. Top to bottom, left to right, an electric pencil sharpener, a snake, a roll of drafting tape, triangles, an architect's scale ruler, a circle template, a drafting brush, scissors, Pink Pearl Eraser, erasing shield, stapler, tape dispenser, drafting dots, electric eraser.*

There is a raised straight edge, a strip of plastic twelve inches long and two inches wide that is supported at each end by wooden blocks three-eighths of an inch high. Its purpose is to draw long, straight lines that look as if they were freehanded. Because the pencil rests against an elevated edge, it is possible to put a little wiggle into straight lines drawn with this instrument.

My drawer also includes a snake. It assumes any curve whatsoever and serves as a guide for drawing lines. The snake is useful in site plans for delineating roads and sidewalks with compound curves.

## Paper Stock

*I have a horror of a white sheet of paper. It creates such a disagreeable impression that it makes me sterile, even ridding me of my taste for work.*

ODILON REDON

There are three primary factors to consider in selecting a paper: its tooth, texture, and weight. If even one of these attributes of the paper is not in agreement with the pencil, the drawing experience risks degenerating into an unruly affair.

The tooth of the paper, its "bite," affects the rate at which the pencil delivers graphite to the surface of the paper. A paper with a coarse tooth, analogous to sandpaper, is ideal for large renderings where detail is not important and the goal is to cover broad areas efficiently. A paper with very little tooth, like photocopy paper, may be desirable in situations where we want complete control over the finest detail of our linework. The texture of the paper's tooth also affects the look of areas of even pencil tone. Some papers, like certain blueprint paper, have an inconsistent textural surface. The fibers of the surface break down under the pressure of the pencil stroke.

Paper weight becomes a factor if we want to trace our images. The lighter the weight, the easier it is to see through the paper. Weight also affects the susceptibility of the paper to denting, to the buildup of valleys

in the paper due to the pressure of the pencil point. If copying, not tracing images, a heavy paper weight is recommended.

Some illustrators also consider the paper's durability over time, its archival qualities. Due to their high acid content, ordinary drawing papers, like newsprint, have a tendency to yellow and deteriorate with age. Unless otherwise specified by the manufacturer, we must assume that the paper we select for our drawings will break down over time.

There are many different kinds of paper stock (Figure 1–4). Yellow tracing paper, for example, which is purchased in rolls as opposed to individual sheets, takes pencil very well. It has a good medium tooth with slightly more bite than vellum. Its major drawback is its weight. Tracing paper is lightweight, very thin, and therefore, prone to tearing.

Vellum provides a durable working surface with a good, subtle tooth. Somewhat heavier than tracing paper, it is nonetheless very translucent, making it ideal for tracing purposes. A finished rendering on vellum, if dry-mounted on a white surface, can be very striking. A translucent paper like vellum, if not dry-mounted flush to its backing, will reveal shadows of its own linework on the surface backing it. Vellum is available in sheets or rolls.

Mylar, a kind of translucent drawing plastic, has a razor-sharp tooth. Because its tooth is so sharp, it is difficult on this surface to control the subtle pencil pressures required to achieve a full range of tonal variation.

There are many different brands of artist's sketch pads on the market today. Aquabee, Strathmore, and Bienfang, to name a few, manufacture fine quality drawing paper. The Bienfang Studio Series No. 501-CL is a good medium-weight paper with a gentle tooth. Many drawings in this book were done on Strathmore Alexis paper, a brand no longer manufactured. Alexis was replaced by Strathmore 400 Series drawing paper. Other types of paper to consider include photo barrier paper, which has a medium tooth and is very inexpensive, and Stonehenge, a high quality paper with an excellent tooth.

A few of the drawings in the book were done on inexpensive photocopy paper (Figures 2–7, 9–2, 9–15). Because it is lightweight, photocopy paper is adaptable to tracing with a light table and, because it has very little tooth, reveals little evidence of its own texture in a finished rendering. Its fibers will not come loose under the pressure of the pencil. This is understandable in light of the need for the photocopy machine itself to remain free of the buildup of fibrous material.

*Figure* 1–4.　*It is always a pleasure to feel the different textures of various drawing papers.*

# Model-Making Equipment

Model-making is an integral part of the renderer's craft (Figure 1–5). The task of drawing complex physical terrain, for example, is made easier if we first construct a physical model of the proposed site. Modelled stage sets, such as those described in chapter seven of this book, are also useful for rendering purposes. The following equipment is beneficial in constructing models.

The knife is an important tool, of which there are three types. The most primitive and brutal type is the utility knife. There are two varieties of utility knife. One has a removeable, retractable blade; the other, a long, single retractable blade that can be broken off at equal intervals in order to expose a new, sharp blade. These knives are great for cutting long, straight lines. Here, the snap-off type blade is expedient and convenient. All utility knives have two major drawbacks. First, they're lousy for cutting tight curves. Second, the thickness of these blades, and likewise the angle of the blade's ground cutting edge, typically generates an angled cut on thicker construction materials. The results of this are angled edges that are not perpendicular to the cutting surface, and butted joints that are not as clean as they could otherwise be.

The second kind of knife, the X-Acto knife, accepts a wide range of blades. Some of these blades are long and narrow, others swivel, while still others resemble miniature meat cleavers. The blade of choice in model making is the No. 11 blade, the one that comes to a long, elegant point. This blade's biggest asset is it can cut tight curves such as those found in landscape contours. Its disadvantages include its poor straight-line cutting ability, the delicate and brittle nature of the sharp tip (it breaks off), and its susceptibility to quick dulling.

The third type of knife, if it can be called this, is the single-sided razor blade. This blade is reserved for the true modelling aficionado; it cuts clean and straight, and its thinness virtually eliminates the bevelled-edge problem typical of utility knives. In spite of these advantages, some people consider the razor blade dangerous; the small, thin handle, combined with a long, sharp, flexible blade, pose a constant potential threat to the model-maker's fingertips.

Other essential equipment includes glue, straight edge/ruler, and cutting surface. A good white glue, such as the household Elmer's glue, is quite effective for landscape model construction. While electric hot glue guns are handy, the glue sets in a quick and inconvenient fashion. Therefore, glue guns are best for use on rough study models rather than refined finished models.

The best ruler to use is a metal cork-backed type. The metal doesn't succumb to a knife's menacing edge and the cork backing prevents the ruler from slipping.

Cutting surfaces are available in many sizes and shapes, at various costs. Some surfaces, such as the self-healing cutting mat, are specifically designed for model-making. Although superior in performance to other cutting surfaces, these mats can be expensive. Less expensive surfaces include masonite, chipboard, and particle board. Avoid cutting surfaces that exhibit any hint of grain, such as plywood, corrugated cardboard, and solid wood. The reasoning here is that a knife can ride the grain of the surface, resulting in a cut other than that which the modeller intended. The key is control of the blade, directing its cut and maintaining its sharp edge. The most picayune model-makers use razor blades as the knife of choice on a glass surface.

## Camera Equipment

A 35-mm camera equipped with a 55-mm macro-lens is useful for taking photographs of landscape models (Figure 1–6). Images may be developed into slides or photographs. For tracing purposes, slides are enlarged with the aid of a slide projector and light table; photographs may be enlarged on photocopy machines to produce color transparencies.

## Light Tables

The simplest of these is not actually a table at all. For the purpose of directly tracing images, a slab of 1/4" thick glass backed by a convenient light source will do. For the purpose of tracing images from slides, a typical light table setup includes a slide projector with a mirror beneath the light table, angled appropriately to project an image onto the underside of a transparent or translucent drawing surface (Figure 1–7).

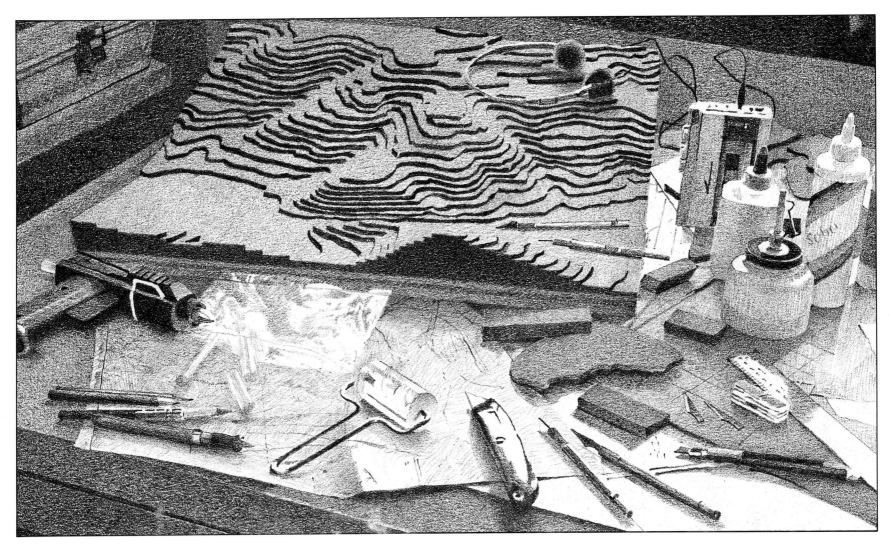

*Figure 1–5.*   *Model-making is an integral part of the renderer's craft.*

*Figure* 1–6.    *A common type of camera is the 35-mm SLR.*

*Figure* 1–7.    *It is essential that all renderers own light tables.*

**Figure 1–8.** *"Haven't you had enough with that computer?" cried the old artist, grinding his false teeth and stamping his wrinkled feet.*

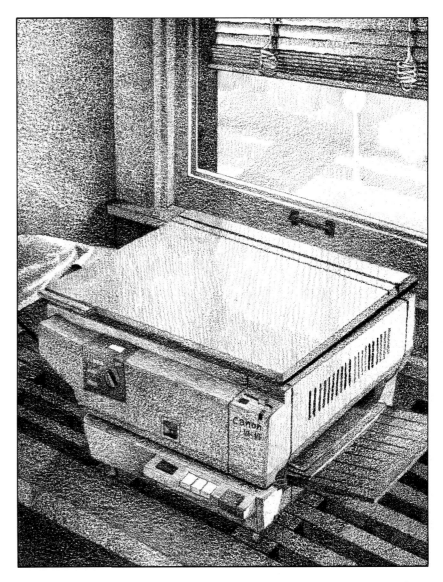

**Figure 1–9.** *The most useful, if not the least appreciated, piece of expensive equipment in the office is the photocopy machine.*

## Computer Equipment

The computer is revolutionizing the way that we model buildings in the landscape (Figure 1–8). Using Computer Aided Design (CAD) software, the renderer is now able to model the structure of virtually any three-dimensional form with comparative ease.

## Photocopier

Photocopied images are either traced as base drawings or rendered directly. The direct application of pencil to photocopy is often recommended for preliminary studies and design drawings, but is not recommended for final rendered presentations (Figure 1–9).

## The Indoor Working Environment

*A rain-tight roof, frugal living, a box of colors, and . . . sunlight through clear windows keep the soul attuned and the body vigorous for one's daily work.*

ALBERT PINKHAM RYDER

For best pencil rendering results, a well-lighted workspace is essential (Figure 1–10). The better this lighting, the less likely it is for us to be caught by surprise when we first glimpse our work under the fullness of broad daylight. The drawing paper should be illuminated by a source that will not cast shadows upon the drawing area. Lighting from too many sources at one time may generate shadow complexities as well as reflections on the drawing surface. For artificial lighting, the movable architect's lamp, with its hinges and swivel base, works well.

A grow lamp, (i.e., a lamp designed for use on plants and flowers), instead of a conventional incandescent bulb is suggested as the source of illumination for the architect's swivel lamp. With conventional incandescent bulbs, a pronounced yellow bias in the spectral range of the illuminating lamp bathes color renderings in warmer light, thereby deceiving the renderer into believing that the drawing is warmer than it actually is. This becomes apparent when the finished rendering is finally viewed in natural sunlight. The grow lamp averts this problem. Color shifts may also be averted by using both incandescent and fluorescent lights when rendering under artificial lighting conditions.

With regard to natural daylighting, north light is desirable. Sunlight through windows facing other than north will pour in at some time during the day, creating objectionable shadows and reflections on the surface of the drawing. North light is reflected light, provided indirectly, and it therefore casts softer, less intrusive shadows on the drawing paper's surface. This light is more constant than light from other directions.

A primary consideration in deciding upon a drawing table is its ability to tilt to different angles. Ideally, we should be able to view our drawings head on. Our view of the rendering should not be distorted due to foreshortening. If the drawing is fixed to a horizontal viewing surface, the renderer must constantly lean over the table to view the drawing frontally. If the drawing can be positioned vertically, the illustrator has the option of viewing the work frontally, without having to lean over the board.

**Figure** 1–10.    *A well-lighted workspace brings every pencil stroke to life.*

## On Drawing Outdoors

Winslow Homer believed that painting should not be done indoors. "Outdoors," he said, "you have the sky providing one light, you have the reflected light of reflective surfaces, and the direct light of the sun. In the blending of these light sources, there is not a line to be found anywhere in the drawing." The Impressionist painters, too, sought their truth in natural settings rather than in the confines of the studio. Monet himself had "no other wish than a close fusion with nature, and I desire no other fate than (according to Goethe's precept) to have worked and lived in harmony with her laws."

In the specialized field of painting, one of the principle aims of the Impressionist movement was to depict nature spontaneously. Thus, Impressionism represented an approach toward art that lent itself little to analysis or reflection. For our purposes, the romantic notion that drawing is a product of immediate inspiration runs against the grain of the reasoned and reflective analysis required to study natural forms for their nuances in detail. Outdoors, the sun constantly changes position, affecting the disposition of shade and shadow in our drawings; the clouds are in motion, the leaves on the trees are not always still, trucks suddenly pull up and park in the middle of our compositions. There is the constant threat of rain, and then there are the people who drift in and out of the picture and those who gather round to look over our shoulders, offering advice on work in progress.

Edgar Degas thought that artists (particularly Impressionists) working out of doors ought to be monitored by shotgun-wielding militia men who could issue "a little dose of bird shot now and then as a warning." This book advocates visiting a place first-hand, then "capturing the moment" with a photo. Rather than sketch outdoors (Figure 1–11), it's much more comfortable to reflect on the nuances of a scene indoors, under consistent weather and lighting conditions.

**Figure 1–11.** *After a day's hike through virgin regions of northern Wisconsin wilderness, the sketch artist arrived at a small clearing near a pond.*

# Chapter 2

# The Second Simple Pleasure of Rendering: Applying Pencil to Paper

*Then I want to do something very modest; to work out by myself a tiny, formal motive, one that my pencil will be able to hold without any formal technique.*

PAUL KLEE

*The surface, at times raised to the highest pitch of liveliness, should transmit to the beholder the sensation which possessed the artist.*

ALFRED SISLEY

*I don't think it would be more ridiculous for a person to put his nose close to the canvas and say the colors smell offensive than to say how rough the paint lies . . .*

THOMAS GAINSBOROUGH

It's easy to draw. Just grab the pencil and lay down some lead; or so it would seem. This non-method of depositing graphite on paper may be appropriate for pencil sketching, where refinement of technique is an open-ended question. But the rendering, which is a delicately executed piece of work, is a different matter altogether. Within its exacting tolerances, even the subtlest nuance of a single pencil stroke reveals a little of the renderer's character.

The heavy hand, for example, ignores the surface of the paper by digging trenches through its tooth. As these dark pencil troughs begin to accumulate on paper, a picture emerges, and with it evidence of a larger, sinister plot. The heavy hand clears away the surface of the drawing paper in much the same way that an asphalt contractor clears the land to make way for a parking lot. The ultimate goal of the heavy hand is to blot out the entire surface of the paper in an effort to create an image so real that we would be tempted to thrust our arm through the drawing just to make sure that it was in fact only an illusion.

By contrast, the light hand worries about disturbing even the subtle grain of a fine-tooth rendering paper. Pencil graphite merely nicks the paper's tooth, adhering to it more by accident than by choice. If we lifted a light-handed rendering by one of its corners and gently shook it in a breeze, the meager accumulation of lead on the paper's surface would certainly fall like dust to the pavement.

The sensitive hand develops an awareness of the very subtle sensation that may be felt as the pencil's graphite is pulled over the paper's tooth. Pencil marks laid down in such a way reveal the delineator's appreciation of the resonant tension between paper and pencil mark. Each pencil stroke recorded on paper is like the groove of a phonograph record. It may be played back later through the eye of the viewer. The simple act of continuously shearing little wedges of gray graphite from the tip of our sharpened pencil as it rides over the ridges of the tooth of a good drawing paper is one of pencil rendering's little pleasures.

Textures in the surface of the drawing paper of a completed rendering stand in counterpoint to the perceived or imagined depth of the actual composition. The tension between the flat, visible surface and the image in depth, if in balance, suggests a kind of control on the part of the delineator, a control based on the renderer's ability to resolve the conflict between the material facts of the pencil and paper on the one hand and the idea of the pictorial space on the other.

The pattern of pencil strokes sometimes tells a story about the delineator. Some people draw with such a strong flourish that an exaggerated personal style emerges. In extreme cases, this self-consciousness so overwhelms every other aspect of the drawing that it seems quite clear that such artists are not interested in anything other than the shape of their own doodles. Just as disturbing are those renderings which, upon completion, are so stiff and lifeless as to suggest that the delineator's efforts to capture nature as it actually appears were made under fear of censorship.

## Pencil Stroke Techniques

Drawing exercises are intended to acquaint the beginner with the rudimentary technical skills necessary to execute basic renderings (Figure 2–1). A select few of these pencil stroke exercises have become so firmly ingrained in the collective introductory chapters of rendering books that they have become archetypal. Over one hundred years ago, on the topic of how to apply tone on a piece of paper, John Ruskin, for example, in his book, *Elements of Drawing*, advised the reader to draw a grid of small squares, "filling each with closely spaced lines, making some boxes light, others dark." Arthur Guptill, in his classic book, *Rendering in Pencil*, recommends much the same thing. It is common practice today to begin rendering classes with the same exercises advocated by Ruskin.

The basic pencil stroke exercise consists of filling in bands of squares with tone. Beginning with a white square, each successive square is made incrementally darker in tonal value until the final square in the sequence is nearly black. The exercise consists of creating ten squares arranged in equal increments of stepped tonal gradations. With regard to these value scales, it is again worth heeding Ruskin's advice. He cautions against extremes of light and dark. Darks should never be "black nor approaching black, they should be evidently and always of a luminous nature"—an effect achieved by showing a texture of white flecks among the black lines.

Once the tonal value scale has been mastered, it is instructive to recreate these same value scales using different types of line strokes. For example, one value scale might be made up of all diagonal line strokes, another with a patterned line stroke, yet another with a scribbled texture. It is also useful to create scales of gradually changing tones which employ a different line stroke within each square. Pencil stroke exercises may also emphasize various types of pencil point, ranging from dull to sharp. Finally, these exercises are useful in developing skill at depicting surface materials such as brick, grass, stone, or wood.

It should be noted that the words "value" and "tone" are interchangeable throughout the text. Both terms address the relative lightness or darkness of an area of a rendering. Every area of a rendering, whether it is black or white, flat or textured, patterned or chaotic, has a tonal value.

*Figure 2–1.* Inexperienced renderers often are made to fill in little squares.

## Line Quality

The texture of our rendering paper is gradually revealed to us through the tender buildup of pencil strokes. If these pencil strokes are applied with care, in delicate layers, the paper's texture will remain visible across the entire breadth of the rendering to the very end of the drawing process. The rendering will have coherence. Paper texture is subtle. It is often the last attribute of the drawing that the beginning renderer learns to appreciate.

The pencil strokes themselves contribute to the coherence of a rendering. Sometimes, tonal areas are rendered by first smearing graphite across the face of the paper. This graphite is then worked into the paper's tooth with a smudge stick. The result is a tonal area that shines like the dull side of aluminum foil. Drawings rendered in this way feel quick, smooth, and superficial, like their application technique. On the other hand, pencil strokes applied to the surface of the paper with care, one crisp line next to another, appear to the viewer like a finely woven natural fabric. The beauty and coherence of the rendering's surface, it seems, is directly related to the amount of time that we are willing to invest in our pencil textures.

The drawing in Figure 2–2 was rendered using three pencil points: sharp, blunt, and dull. A sharp point was used to delineate the wood grain of the taper of both pencils shown in the rendering. The drawing within the rendering was executed with a blunt pencil point. The tonal buildup in the upper right hand corner of the rendering was crafted with a dull pencil point.

## Luminosity

Distilled water is flat and dull; carbonated water has fizz and sparkle. Dull, flat grays are the distilled water of rendered tonal value. Luminosity carbonates these tonal areas, making them sparkle. The subtlest form of luminosity is made possible through the paper's tooth, which is revealed by little white flecks in the areas of built-up dark tone. These white flecks of paper's tooth are often visible even in the darkest tonal area of high quality pencil renderings.

A more obvious example of luminosity is the crispness of the white spaces between the buildup of our lines. Too often, the beginner ignores the condition of the pencil point during composition. This usually results in blunt or dull lines where sharp lines were desired, thus reducing the level of sparkle in the drawing, dulling its visual allure.

Sometimes, blunt lines are the result of a failure to turn or rotate the pencil between strokes, thereby diminishing the number of sharp lines obtained between pencil sharpenings. Other times, the pencil sharpener itself is nothing more than a meat grinder masquerading as a sharpener. Dull sharpeners give way to avoidance behaviors that contribute to dull pencils. Finally, another cause of blunt lines and smudged tonal areas may be traced to the level of patience of the renderer. The serious renderer realizes that with lack of patience line quality deteriorates.

**Figure 2–2.** *Luminosity is revealed in the thousands of little white flecks of the paper's tooth that appear during the slow buildup of pencil strokes.*

# Edges in Line, Edges in Tone

*Vision changes while it observes. The first, vulgar vision, is that of the simple, dry line, without any attempt at color. In the second stage, the more practiced eye distinguishes delicacies of tone and value; this stage is ahead, less understood by the common eye. The third is that in which the artist sees the multiple subtlety and play of light, its planes, its attractions and directions. These progressive discoveries so modify the primitive vision that line suffers and becomes secondary. This vision will be little understood. It requires long observation and attentive study. . . .*

JAMES ENSOR

Do not use outline around the shape of a tone that is part of a rendering. Outline stands in the way of a tonal rendering like the leaded framework of a stained-glass window. We can read the rendering, but not without a certain pain. The contour drawing depicts figures in outline (Figure 2–3). Finished renderings portray these same features in tone. The cartoonist sketches in line; the artist paints in tone (Figure 2–4). The world as it appears to our eye and as it ought to appear in our renderings is tonal.

Some media naturally lend themselves to tonal representation. The airbrush, for example, lays down broad areas of tone in quick, sweeping flourishes. The paintbrush and the watercolor brush are also primarily instruments for the application of tone. But the pencil, like the pen, is a linear instrument. On first impression, this inherent limitation of the pencil as a linear device would seem to rule it out as medium for developing tonal areas. Far from a problem, however, this shortcoming may actually be turned to advantage. In many refined tonal pencil drawings, the tension between tone and line is deliberate. The stark flatness of certain of the rendering's tones is made to contrast with the visible hint of the buildup of these flat tones through many carefully spaced line strokes. This tension, while difficult and time-consuming to achieve, serves to increase the vividness of the rendering.

From a practical point of view, due to the slowness of the process of building up tonal areas with pencil, it is sensible to gauge the amount of surface area to be covered against the time allotted to complete the drawing. In general, the sharper the pencil point, the narrower will be the line and the more time will be required to create tonal areas. In the case of this book's illustrations, efforts were made to minimize the amount of surface area. Just about every drawing in the book is reproduced at its original scale.

One final note: Avoid the temptation to draw heavy line silhouettes around the shapes of elements depicted in tone. While this rendering device may be effective for mechanically isolating significant contours, it has a tendancy to undermine the rendering's sense of realism.

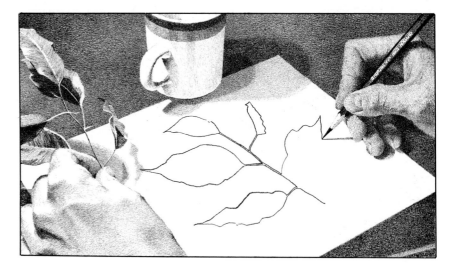

*Figure 2–3.    Contour drawings capture the significant shapes of things. They ignore the textural and tonal possibilities that lurk between the lines.*

**Figure 2–4.** *Cartoonists sketch in line; the artists paint in tone.*

## Working From Photographs

The camera freezes action in a way that makes it possible for us to study, dissect, reflect on things later on. We take a picture so that we can study something as simple as the shadow of a tree on wet pavement. In the photograph, the pavement never dries, the sun angle never changes. Renoir once wrote: "Out of doors there is a greater variety of light than in the studio, where, to all intents and purposes, it is constant; but, for just that reason, light plays too great a part outdoors; you have no time to work out the composition; you can't see what you are doing. If the painter works directly from nature, he ultimately looks for nothing but momentary effects; he does not try to compose, and soon he gets monotonous."

Assuming that we don't work directly from nature, then what are we to do? Indoors we have two options. We either copy or trace from photographs. Each option involves a different kind of rendering process and emphasizes the development and refinement of different rendering skills.

## Copying Photographs

Copying from photographs of places that we visit develops our skill at contour and outline drawing. It hones our ability to proportion things. The difficult part of copying from a picture is getting shapes down on paper. One way to solve this problem is to grid both the photograph and the paper into proportionally equal divisions and then transfer shapes from photo to paper based on the intersection of shapes with grid lines. It should be noted, however, that this gridding procedure defeats the purpose of copying in the first place. By gridding, we lose a bit of the humanizing charm of forms and lines not quite true to the ruthless standards of the camera's lens.

The copied drawing's tonality is built from the lightest values to the darkest, in layers.

## Tracing Photographs

Traced drawings are built up in several pencil layers, from the darkest value to the lightest.

Blurred edges and subtle tonal gradations are difficult to trace. In these cases, it is common practice to first trace general shapes and tones. Tonal values can be refined later by copying from the photograph.

Figure 2–5 was illustrated as follows: A 3 × 5 photo was enlarged on a color copying machine to fit an 8 $\frac{1}{2}$ × 11 transparency. The transparency was taped to a square sheet of glass. Drawing paper was taped over the transparency. The image was backlit and traced.

**Figure 2–5.**    *Illustrated is the technique for illustrating the illustration.*

# Modelling Form

The pencil is a linear medium. It applies tone to paper in thin strands, like wire. The question naturally arises, which direction should we draw our pencil lines to indicate the form of objects? Are there any rules or guidelines that we should follow? Generally speaking, no. Individual pencil strokes may be laid down to highlight several different qualities of the rendering, including its subject matter, the artist, the paper, or a prevailing style. It is even possible to lay down pencil strokes to contradict the content of the rendering.

By convention, pencil strokes create three different effects: painted, screened, or modelled. The painted effect is achieved through a massive buildup of graphite on the surface of the paper, resulting in a picture that is indistinguishable from a photograph. This effect is not discussed in the text.

The screen effect is achieved by laying down pencil strokes parallel to each other across the entire surface of the rendering, so that the drawing looks as if its subject matter is viewed through a diagonal screen. The screen effect does not mold the form of individual objects. Parallel line strokes are usually drawn at 45 degrees. The specific direction of this angle is dependent upon whether the render is left or right handed. An example of this effect is illustrated in Figure 2–6. The picture within the picture was executed as a screen drawing.

The modelled form effect also incorporates visible line strokes, but they are varied to capture the specific texture or contour of the objects or surfaces delineated. In the modelled form effect, lines conform to shapes; objects depicted hint at the objects' shapes. Curved strokes are recommended for curved surfaces. Likewise, for landscape elements, line strokes are drawn in the direction of plant growth. Grass is typically drawn with vertical lines; low, spreading shrubs with more diagonal lines. Pencil strokes for shadows often indicate the direction of the light source, paralleling the direction of the sun's rays.

The potato and leaf forms in Figure 2–6 were rendered with pencil strokes that conformed to the contour and texture of their surface. Note, in the potato's skin, how the pencil strokes accentuate three attributes of its surface: its shade and shadow, its surface curvature, and its surface texture.

Finally, it is important to study the implications of applying line strokes as they affect the whole of the composition. Before we begin to draw, it is beneficial to develop a strategy that accounts for the type of line strokes we are planning to use in order to express various forms throughout the entire drawing. In this regard, the more the pencil strokes bring out the attributes of contour, texture and light on an object's surface, the more prominent the object will appear in the rendering. On the other hand, the more the object is visually flattened through tonal screening, the less the object will stand out. Elements intended to stand out, to gain visual prominence in the rendering, should receive detailed treatment through pencil strokes sympathetic with the element's contour, texture, and shadow.

**Figure 2–6.**    Note how, in the potato's skin, the pencil strokes accentuate three attributes of its surface: its shade and shadow, its surface curvature, and its surface texture.

## Maintenance of Drawings

Correcting mistakes in our drawings is not limited to a single technique. In fact, the methods that we use for erasing our drawings may vary, depending on the kind of rendering style it is that we are after. If crisp, bright pencil lines are an ingredient of the rendering style, the best way to maintain the drawing is to not make major mistakes. The key to avoiding major mistakes is to think twice before giving up empty areas of the drawing. Once an empty area of the paper is filled with tone, the original whiteness of the paper can only be restored with great difficulty, if at all. Even after extensive erasure, the paper will retain a shiny gray tone, because the paper's tooth will be smoothed flat by the crushing, smearing action of the eraser.

On the other hand, the rendering style may accommodate major erasures. This means sacrificing the goal of achieveing consistent luminosity across the entire surface of the page. But we can easily interpret the effect of a major erasure as something to be sought after rather than avoided, a kind of subtle, spontaneous gesture, a happy accident, intended to relieve the overbearing monotony of consistency. This rendering style gains visual interest through the juxtaposition of smooth, dull, erased areas with brighter, unerased areas, creative tension beneath the even, consistent application of a final layer of pencil strokes. Figure 9–26 includes a major erasure.

For small area mistakes I use an erasing shield with either a "Pink Pearl" or "Rub Kleen" eraser. For very small mistakes, and as a last-ditch effort, I literally scrape away the error with the sharp tip of an X-acto knife. In Figure 6–3, the point of the knife was used extensively to repair a dull area of the drawing.

Sometimes, the rendering is complete but the overall tonal balance requires adjustment. In these situations, I use a kneaded eraser to selectively dab away tonal value. In Figure 2–7, the tonal value of the trees in the picture was too dark. The trees were lightened in value by pressing a kneaded eraser to the areas in need of tonal reduction.

Finally, I spray fix finished renderings, if only to prevent smudging. A workable spray fixative is recommended. Many of the illustrations in this book were worked over after they had been spray fixed. Figure 4–5 is an example of a drawing that was reworked extensively. Fixative may retard but cannot eliminate the dreaded waxy bloom, the whitish film that gradually haunts wax pencil drawings. Fixative will also subtly change the intensity of certain colors.

**Figure 2–7.** *With the help of a kneaded eraser, the delineator's calm, intelligent hand wrestled to save the lusterless rendering.*

# Chapter 3

# Depicting Trees and Other Landscape Features

*If I isolate a tree in the landscape, if I approach that tree, I see that its bark has an interesting design and a plastic form; that its branches have dynamic violence which ought to be observed; that its leaves are decorative.*

FERNAND LÉGER

*So rich and fleecy were the outlines of the forest that scarce an opening could be seen, the whole visible earth, from the rounded mountaintop to the water's edge, presenting one unvaried hue of unbroken verdure.*

JAMES FENIMORE COOPER, *The Deerslayer*

*When the dreary heath is spread before the eye and ideas of wilderness and desolation are required, what more suitable accompaniment can be imagined than the blasted oak, ragged, scathed and leafless, shooting its peeled white branches athwart the gathering blackness of some rising storm.*

SIR UVEDALE PRICE

The bark on the trunk of the sugar maple in my back yard is deeply fissured. It has a rough, gritty, weatherbeaten feel to it. As I look up from the base of the tree, I can barely see the morning sky through its many branches and leaves. The leaves of this particular tree are pointy, suspended from branches in symmetrical pairs. Each leaf is just about as long as it is wide. As I step away from the tree, I see that its limbs grow upward and outward. From still further away, the whole tree takes on the shape of an oval.

When I first began sketching trees, I drew what I felt was most important about them: their physical wholeness, the known, measurable aspects of their overall shape, size, and texture. The tree was of a piece and whole in reality, and so I depicted it without violating the integrity of its complete appearance. After a while, as I developed my drawing skills, the tree no longer seemed so inviolable, so immutable. It could be near or far, not just in the midground. And when it was near in my drawings, it became a separate study because it no longer resembled what it did further away.

If asked to sketch a tree, a child would probably draw something resembling a round ball on a stick. A knowledgeable renderer, on the other hand, would sketch something much different. Working from life, or as in Figure 3–1, from a photograph of a specific tree image, the renderer would capture the tree in two if not three or more layers, each layer contributing to an overall impression.

The tree, like every other object in the landscape, is complex and varied, and it seems there is no end to the number of questions we may ask about it. In this chapter, rather than focus only on the general attributes of a midground tree seen in its entirety, we shall look at the tree in light of its changing identity in different rendering contexts, including the tree as shadow and the tree as foreground, midground, and background phenomenon.

Multiple layers of complexity also weave their way through water and clouds, other landscape features described in this chapter. Unlike the tree, which may be envisioned as a discrete particular and easily isolated from its context, however, water and clouds have no definite contour, no intrinsic shape. For their sense of identity, both are molded by and dependent on their surroundings.

## How to Render Trees

The individual tree is rendered in pencil in one of three ways (Figure 3–2): As a silhouette, the tree is depicted in profile. Its shape as a whole is outlined and then filled in with a solid tonal value. In three value planes, the tree is rendered in white for sunlight, black or dark gray for shadow, and medium gray for intermediate values. The summer trees illustrated in Figure 3–3 were drawn in three tonal planes. Full tonal gradation is the most labor-intensive approach of the three. This method may result in trees that are too visually dominant.

## A Few Tips on Rendering Trees

Tree trunks are seldom as bulky, vertical, and obvious as they appear in our first attempts at rendering them. In many cases, our earliest renderings of trees are awful. Our initial efforts at depicting the entire tree often is an exercise in solid geometry. The tree canopy tends to look like a ball. In fact, trees appear less noticably round in shape than that. Tree outlines are diffuse, not hard-edged. When sketching trees, consider developing foliage from the middle outward, gradually loosening up the tree's leaf boundary with each succeeding layer. That way, the tree's silhouette does not appear solid.

Another problem in the early phase of learning to draw is that the branches of our trees seldom overlap. In reality, many branches of the tree do overlap, a characteristic that should not be exaggerated when depicting midground trees. Too much emphasis on overlap through tonal contrast

results in hyper-three-dimensional-looking trees. In fact, the tonal value of overlapping branches is nearly identical.

## Tree Character

Just as it is possible to categorize buildings on the basis of their architectural style, so, too, is it possible to identify trees on the basis of their species. Factors to consider in making basic distinctions between tree species include the tree's overall height, texture, and shape. The sugar maple, for example, has a spreading form. It has dense foliage, medium texture, and reaches 75 feet in height. The white oak, on the other hand, has a rounded form with wide, spreading, horizontal branches. It has a short trunktop and reaches 100 feet in height. The pin oak is pyramidal in form, densely branched with a straight tapering central stem. It has a dense foliage and reaches 75 feet in height. The Japanese pagoda has a round head on a short trunk and reaches 70 feet in height. All of these trees are illustrated in Figure 3–4. From left to right, top: Sugar maple, white oak; bottom: pin oak, Japanese pagoda tree.

*Figure 3–1.* *"What does the tree look like?," a question frequently asked by the rendering novitiate, is answered definitively by collecting and copying tree portraits.*

**Figure 3–2.** *From the bottom, the same grouping of trees is illustrated in three different ways: (1) as silhouette, (2) in three value planes, and (3) in full tonal gradation.*

## Foreground Trees

The tree as foreground framing was a favorite device in the idyllic landscape paintings of Claude Lorrain, Nicolas Poussin, and Salvator Rosa. In their landscapes, the giant, leaning foreground tree was often positioned between the viewer's eye and the light of the sun. The tree's dark silhouette allowed the sun's rays to bathe the midground scene.

The blatant, theatrical use of such strong foreground framing in an architectural or landscape rendering of today, however, would probably be viewed with suspicion. So would the use of any other foreground element contrived to evoke an obvious mood. The weeping willow, for example, has pendulous branches that all too easily impart feelings of melancholy and nostalgia. Unless such a device is handled in a way that gives new meaning to an old cliche, say, by depicting the willow so that we can literally see the breeze on the pale underside of its leaves, the emotional effect will not ring true. The foreground tree ought also to be environmentally compatible with the other landscape features in the scene. We associate the willow with river banks, and it would indeed be strange to see a willow enframing a view of cactus in the desert.

If the goal of the rendering is a completely honest depiction of its subject, it makes sense to study trees in up close for nuances in their botanical form and detail. A few general observations are in order here. First of all, tree trunks are seldom absolutely vertical. They often lean a few degrees in one direction or another. Often, trees rendered without any slant bear a stronger resemblance to lampposts than to trees. Furthermore, in broad daylight, the dark shadow of one tree branch may fall on another branch, creating a shadow ring (Figure 3–4). Dark limbs in the shadow of the tree's foliage may appear behind lighter limbs, or the other way around. Tree branches overlap (Figure 3–5). Some branches in perspective foreshorten. The pattern of branching and bark varies from one species to another.

## Tree Shadows

On bright summer afternoons, the shadows of tall elms would fall on the houses and sidewalks along the street in the old neighborhood where I lived. Scrambled patterns of sunlight would leak through the tree's deep shadows, animating white porches and green lawns. People walking down the sidewalk appeared as if they were continually changing their clothes. Architectural delineators seldom let the shadows of trees dance on the walls and pitched roofs of the buildings they draw. Perhaps this is due to fear that shadows would mask or obscure a true perception of form. But this is rarely the case. If we follow a few simple rules regarding the pattern of tree shadows on flat surfaces, our renderings will benefit from their inclusion.

The penumbra increases with distance. This diffusing or doubling up of the shadow's edge is evident in Figure 3–6: note its subtle blurring as it gets farther from the tree. The shadow is sharp and crisp as it steps over the curb and into the street. From there, it undergoes a gradual loss of tonal and detail definition, literally appearing to wash out with distance. Note also the change in value of the tree's shadow as it falls in mown grass, then concrete, and finally on asphalt. The shadow seems transparent.

The intensity of the shadow falls off as distance from its source increases. In Figure 3–7, two shadows overlap on a white garage door. The darker, sharper shadow belongs to the tree that is closer to the garage door.

The tree's pattern of sunlight and shadow varies depending on whether

**Figure** 3–3. *Trees rendered in three tonal planes. Traced from* Trees for Architecture and the Landscape, *by Robert L. Zion, pages 22 and 23. From left to right, top: Sugar maple, white oak; bottom: pin oak; Japanese pagoda tree.*

*Figure 3–4.* *In broad daylight, the dark shadow of one tree branch may fall upon another, creating a shadow ring.*

*Figure 3–5.* *Tree branches overlap. Some branches foreshorten. The pattern of branching and bark varies from one species to another.*

it is cast upon receding or normal perspective surfaces. Sunlight holes in the shadow pattern of a tree are usually, although not always, somewhat oval. These ovals conform to the perspective foreshortening of the surface receiving the shadow. Sun ovals remain constant on frontal planes and appear to elongate vertically on planes receding into depth. They do not appear on glass.

The shadow of trees in summer is dominated by the pattern of leaf massing. However, it should be noted that often the pattern of branching is also evident in these shadows. For trees in winter, the shadows of branches appear to overlap. Often, the beginner does not indicate overlap

in the shadow of tree branches. The shadows of branches change perspective with each change in orientation of the surface receiving the shadows.

Shadow patterns vary among tree species. The honey locust casts a much softer, more diffuse shadow than the horse chestnut. When in doubt, it is advisable to let small patches of sunlight play in broad shadows rather than sprinkle bits of shadow amidst the sunlit surfaces.

Finally, it makes no sense to depict tree shadows where they could not occur naturally. If the scene has no trees, or if a tree could not possibly cast a shadow on a wall in the way that we would like it to, then a shadow should not be included on that wall.

**Figure 3–6.** *Tree shadows, as they shift from grass to pavement, blur with increasing distance from the tree.*

## Near and Far Trees

In Figure 3–8, the craggy, occasionally torn texture of a lone foreground object suggests the characteristics of a tree, its bark shedding, its trunk knotted. Just beyond this tree, the nearly vertical shaft of yet another graceful specimen punctuates the rendering's middle distance. In the background, far beyond the translucent leaf canopy of a honey locust, we see a treeline, the park's distant horizontal signature. Trees take on different characters depending on how far they are from the viewer.

To enhance the feeling of depth in a rendering, trees at different locations within the pictorial depth of space are drawn with varying amounts of detail. The bark of the tree in the foreground of Figure 3–8 was rendered with such vivid tonal and textural detail that the viewer could imagine literally touching it. Both midground trees, on the other hand, are rendered with comparatively less detail. The sun is hidden behind early morning clouds, so the shadows are diffuse at the base of these two midground trees. Note the flat tonal treatment of the farther midground tree. No attempt was made to round it into an artificial three-dimensional sphere.

By comparison, the pencil treatment of the background trees is minimal. In the distance of the pictorial space, the shape of each individual tree is only hinted at. However, note that even within the tonal constancy of these distant trees, a variety of subtly different pencil strokes was used.

The foreground often requires more time to render than the background. The extreme foreground tree in Figure 3–8 was drawn in three hours, whereas the entire woodline in the background required only about thirty minutes.

The effects of depth of pictorial field are an important aspect of this rendering. Depth filters out contrasts. The foreground contains more contrasts of texture, tone, shade, shadow, and form than the background, which tends toward uniform gray. Depth also filters out verticals. In theory, the horizon line subsumes all verticals. In an article entitled "The Nomenclature of Pictorial Art," published by the *Art-Union* in 1844, J. B. Pyne wrote: "The [horizontal and perpendicular] possess all the elements of pictorial harmony, that is, relation on some points, and opposition on others, with subordination of one to the other: the horizontal is indicative of a universal law of nature, that of a general subsistence and repose of inanimate matter; and the perpendicular, that of power and action to preserve its position; added to which the horizontal is its own base, being a subsistence of all other lines in nature, while the perpendicular requires one."

**Figure** 3–7.    *Tree shadows drench the garage door in a star-shower of light holes. The tree that is closer to the garage door casts the darker, sharper shadow.*

## Textural Landscape Features

In the wilds of nature, trees and other landscape features blend together. This interconnectedness of uncultivated organic growth is evident along the banks of rivers, in woodlands and forests, even in the desert. It is only through the intervention of man or beast, i.e., the lawn appliance of the former or the grazing of the latter, that the continuous flow of landscape is hideously transformed into neatly organized sections.

The rendition of pure textural vegetation might seem like a complicated and difficult task. In fact, it is not. The eye of the spectator glides easily over areas of changing texture and constant tone. If we hold the tonal value of our textures constant, and if we keep the grain of the texture fairly uniform, even the most entangled pattern of textures can be made to hold together visually in our renderings.

In Figure 3–9, the irregularity and variety of background textures is visually held together through the device of tonal constancy. A squint of the eye reduces the rendering to a primitive blur of tonal contrasts. In this simplified visual blur, the texture of the background vegetation fuses together into a medium-gray tonal value.

## Theatrical Compositions

The scene in Figure 3–9 is more theatrical than natural in appearance. It seems "staged," as if lights were brought in by a movie company in order to backlight the bridge. The pair of hands in the foreground might belong to a movie director framing the shot of a romantic love scene. The many details of the rendering, its individual twigs and blades of grass, are lit in a theatrical way to enhance the overall impression of the shapes within the pictorial space as a whole. Tonal contrasts are deliberately grouped so as to heighten the spatial effect.

In Figure 3–9, the rendering's dominant tonal contrast is located toward the center of the composition, where the dark silhouette of the bridge stands out against the lighter texture of the floor of the ravine. A less intense tonal contrast was used for the drawing's framing device, the hands in the foreground.

## Tonal Counterchange

In order to ensure that the foreground hands advanced visually against the background, the device of tonal counterchange was used. Tonal counterchange involves deliberately graduating the tone of an area so that its edges sharply contrast with the adjacent area. Counterchange is often used by delineators to enhance the sense of visual separation between objects. In Figure 3–9, the bottom of the left thumb was darkened so that it would stand out against the lighter background. The fingers were lightened so that they would stand out against the darker area behind them.

Tonal contrasts can be arranged hierarchically to establish the relative importance of various features in the drawing. Note that the intensity of tonal contrast which sets the hands apart from other features in the rendering is not as great as between the silhouette of the bridge and its background.

**Figure 3–8.** *Rising mist announces a hot summer day, obscuring the distant treeline. Foregrounds attend to detail while backgrounds blend into harmonious generalizations.*

**Figure 3–9.** *Human hands, inherently smooth, contrast in texture with a background thicket of miscellaneous ragged greenery.*

*Figure 3–10. Lake reflecting two eras of European history.*

*Figure 3–11. Fox River homesteads, Appleton, Wisconsin.*

## Water

Because it is a clear liquid with no intrinsic character, water assumes multiple identities. Its many guises include the falling of the waterfall, the running of the river or stream, the rippling of small ponds, the stillness of the reflecting pool, the misting and jetting of the fountain, and the breaking of ocean waves on the beach. There is even the frozen water of the winter northern lake.

In the four scenes depicted in Figures 3–10 through 3–13, the water is still, or nearly so. In each rendering, the most important attribute of the water is not its color but its reflectiveness.

## Reflections in Still Water

*A piece of calm water always contains a picture in itself, an exquisite reflection of the objects above it. If you give the time necessary to draw these reflections, disturbing them here and there as you see the breeze or current disturb them, you will get the effect of water. . . . The picture in the pool needs nearly as much delicate drawing as the picture above the pool.*

JOHN RUSKIN

Images reflect vertically on the surface of a body of water. If the water is as flat as a mirror, which is sometimes the case in early morning, a

*Figure 3–12.*   *Pantheon at Stourhead Garden, Witshire, England.*

*Figure 3–13.*   *Milwaukee skyline from Lake Park Lagoon.*

rendering of the scene may be viewed upside down: the reflected image will look as crisp as the objects that are reflected, although somewhat darker.

But the perfectly smooth reflective surface rarely occurs in nature. A gentle breeze, the drop of a leaf, or the movement of a boat through the water will create ripples. The length of the reflected image is affected by these wave disturbances. As a rule of thumb, the length of reflections of vertical elements such as buildings and trees increases with wave intensity. As these reflections lengthen, they also begin to break apart, as if the pure reflection were cut into horizontal strips with scissors and then pasted to the rendering with gaps between each strip. On the other hand, the length of the reflection shortens if the object casting the reflection is pushed back at an angle to the spectator's view.

The gentle wave action of water is usually depicted in eye-level per-spectives with horizontal lines that are broken at irregular intervals. The eye-level perspective view in Figure 6–1 depicts water with horizontal lines. A localized gust of wind often disrupts the perfect reflective clarity of otherwise still water in medium-sized lakes, reflecting pools, and ponds. The glare of sunlight reflecting on the plane of the water's surface has the effect of completely bleaching out its surface.

In its broadest interpretation, water's reflectiveness impacts on the mood of the depicted scene. For pools, lakes, and ponds, we may distin-guish between two basic effects, one gloomy, the other cheery. The water feels gloomy if not reflective of the sky. If this effect is not desired, the usual procedure is to let light onto the water by removing the dark re-flections of surrounding trees. This is shown in Figures 3–10 through 3–13.

**Figure** 3–14. *Through clean early morning air, the vaporous contours of a scumbled cloud canopy are clearly visible.*

***Figure*** 3–15.    *A carefully rendered atmosphere provides moody setting for London's Big Ben.*

**Figure 3–16.** *Artificial weather: the renderer transforms an otherwise limpid, pale sky into the stone-colored portrait of an impending storm. See Figure 3–12 for comparison.*

## Further Complications of Still Water

*When you are drawing shallow or muddy water, you will see shadows on the bottom, or on the surface, continually modifying the reflections. . . . The more you look down into the water, the better you see objects through it; the more you look along it, the eye being low, the more you see the reflection of objects above it.*

JOHN RUSKIN

The angle at which we view the water's surface affects its degree of reflectiveness. The more our viewing angle of the water parallels its surface, the more the water acts as a mirror. On the other hand, the more head-on we view the water's surface, the more we see through it. Our view of foreground water is more perpendicular than our view of water in background. Foreground water is therefore more transparent and less reflective than background water. Because the bottom of a pond or lake is usually dark and muddy, the water rendered in the foreground assumes the tonal value of mud. With increasing distance into the perspective view, that is, as the angle of our view becomes more parallel to the water's surface, the water is more reflective, assuming the properties of a mirror.

Finally, the clarity of the water affects its capacity to receive shadows. We may see the shadows of trees and other landscape features on the surface of muddy water, but these same shadows would not appear on the surface of clear water.

## Clouds

Clouds are difficult to render in pencil partly because they have specific shapes yet they have no definite edges. This difficulty is compounded by the fact that in most situations, the renderer must depict the shapes that are not there. When clouds are lighter in value than the background sky, the renderer must draw the darker negative shapes of the background sky, not the lighter positive shapes of the diffusely shaped cloud figures. All of this frustration is compounded by the fact that the really beautiful cloudy skies exhibit complex layering patterns (Figures 3–14, 3–15). One solution to the cloud-rendering problem is to render the sky in flat tones. Clear, sunny skies are a reasonable alternative, as are uniform gray tonal treatments of the sky (Figure 3–16).

In general, clouds gather into horizontal bands toward the horizon. This banding in the distance is in counterpoint to the amorphous, lumpy look of clouds as they appear directly overhead. Clouds drift across the sky in definite formations (Figure 3–17). There's the high, distant, streaky cirrus formation, the billowing cumulus formation below that, the still lower stratus formation, and the long, low, gray layer which uniformly covers the sky. Although clouds are difficult to capture in form, they are quite easy to capture in tone. One technique for drawing clouds consists of two steps. First, the sky is smeared with an even layer of graphite. Then, with a kneaded eraser, portions of the sky are selectively removed to create the shapes of the clouds. Other dry media that work effectively for this purpose include chalk and pastel.

*Figure 3–17.  Miscellaneous cloud formations. The top row shows cirrus formations, the bottom row illustrates variations of alto cumulus clouds.*

# Chapter 4

# Plan Graphics

Site plans are like maps. They are aerial overviews looking straight down on landscapes. Site plans show the measured plan relationships between selected ground features.

Pictorial realism, a sought-after attribute of the eye-level perspective view, is not often a concern in the rendered site plan. If it were, we would be compelled to include in the plan not just all of the trees, but all of the water, the effects of the sun and wind, and maybe even traces of low-lying clouds passing between spectator above and landscape below. The plan's realism would be complete when the viewer of the drawing felt as if he were looking at an aerial photograph. All of these embellishments would be necessary in order to invoke the classic suspension of disbelief deemed so important in engaging the viewer of a good perspective scene.

But this heightened sense of realism could easily render the site plan useless as a navigational instrument. Roads and paths would be hidden beneath tree canopies and clouds. We could not see where ground features were located. Because it is primarily intended as a mapping device, the rendered plan is therefore usually abstracted.

This abstraction often takes the form of one or more horizontal sections through the site plan at different elevational heights. Each section reveals something different about the site. The highest horizontal section reveals an overview of the site plan, as if it were being seen from high in the air. From this altitude, configurations of buildings and trees may be seen. A horizontal section taken much lower, just below the canopies of the trees, for example, reveals the pattern of ground cover, water, and paths on the surface. Site contours, lines at constant elevational heights, become visible. A horizontal section taken still further down, just below the surface, reveals not only the foundations of buildings, but also water and tree placement. There would be no evidence of paths.

Even in the face of this abstraction, there is room for realism. There are situations in rendering plans that call for the believable depiction of the trees. Consequently, it is possible to spend quite a lot of time searching for and obtaining photographs of trees and other landscape features as they appear from the sky. But most people only rarely get an aerial view of things, and the need for realism of the sort which is found in a good perspective is not so essential in site plans. To save time and expense, the use of realistic-looking symbolic imagery seems appropriate. This chapter therefore describes conventions to express the various features depicted in site plans.

Selected examples are arranged according to scale.

*Figure 4–1.* *Rendering from aerial photo.*

*Figure 4–2.* *Rendering from aerial photo.*

## Aerial Views

Aerial photographs of landscape features are not easy to find. The cover of a book entitled *All About Landscaping*, by Lin Cotton, published in 1980 by Ortho Books, Chevron Chemical Company Consumer Products Division, ASLA, San Francisco served as the basis for Figures 4–1 and 4–2.

In these two traced aerial views, the leaves of the trees look just as they would if viewed at the same distance from a ground-level perspective. The pattern of leaf massing is visually complex, consisting of stark tonal contrasts of sunlight and shadow. Note that trees do not always read as separate elements. Two broad leaf evergreen trees visually merge. The patterns and textures of low-lying shrubs, bushes, and other forms of ground vegetation are also in evidence, although not as visually prominent as the taller and more massive trees. Site plans of landscapes that do not yet exist can be constructed on the basis of what we learn from studying aerial views firsthand (Figure 4–3).

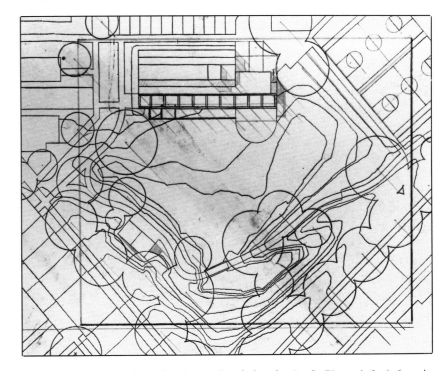

*Figure* 4–4. *Contoured site plan that served as the base drawing for Figures 4–5, 4–6, and 4–7.*

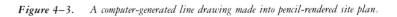

*Figure* 4–3. *A computer-generated line drawing made into pencil-rendered site plan.*

*Figure 4–5.* *Hyper-realistic rendered interpretation (with minor variations) of contoured site plan depicted in Figure 4–4.*

## Rendered Site

The library grounds depicted in contour plan in Figure 4–4 include a pond, a footpath, and numerous trees. The shape of the ground plane is defined with contour lines. Each contour line represents a constant elevational height. This line-drawn contour plan can be rendered more elaborately in several different ways. Three variations are shown (Figures 4–5,

4–6, and 4–7). In the first variation (Figure 4–5), the texture of the ground is smooth; the texture of trees is ragged. Both were painstakingly built up in several layers of pencil strokes. Trees at this scale often appear more flat than round. Their shapes appear to visually fuse together. Note that the value of tree shadows changes as it moves over different surfaces. The drawing's overall pattern of light and dark emphasizes the relative closeness of elements to the viewer. In general, lighter values and stronger tonal contrasts seem to advance toward the eye of the viewer.

Some site plans are brutal and hard-edged (Figure 4–6). There is nothing soft or delicate about trees rendered as if they were flat, white transparent disks, revealing the paths that meander below and between them. The rendering is done in black and white on middle gray. In the plan, white elements appear to advance toward the viewer with respect to the middle gray; dark tones appear to recede. The black shadows not only emphasize the sense of depth in the plan on the basis of their relative lengths, but wherever they are in opposition to white, they also "push" the white areas of the drawing perceptually closer to the viewer's eye. Buildings in the plan appear to advance toward the viewer because they are of a significantly lighter tone than their surroundings.

Trees may have a much freer and more natural feel to them (Figure 4–7). To achieve naturalistic effects, these trees were rendered in layers. The first layer was rendered in a high-contrast black/white texture. It was impossible to create controlled spontaneous patterns of each tree directly in the rendering, so their irregular pattern was made beforehand. Dried weeds were first dipped in ink, then their imprints were stamped on a piece of paper. The best of the imprint patterns were traced in black into the renderings. (Thomas Gainsborough is said to have achieved a sense of spontaneity in his famous landscapes in much the same way. He would do this by dabbing his paintings—he called it "mopping"—with a sponge tied to the end of a stick.) Light gray shadows were then layered over the top of each tree pattern, creating a sense of leaf massing within each of the individual trees. Note that many of the trees appear to overlap or adjoin one another.

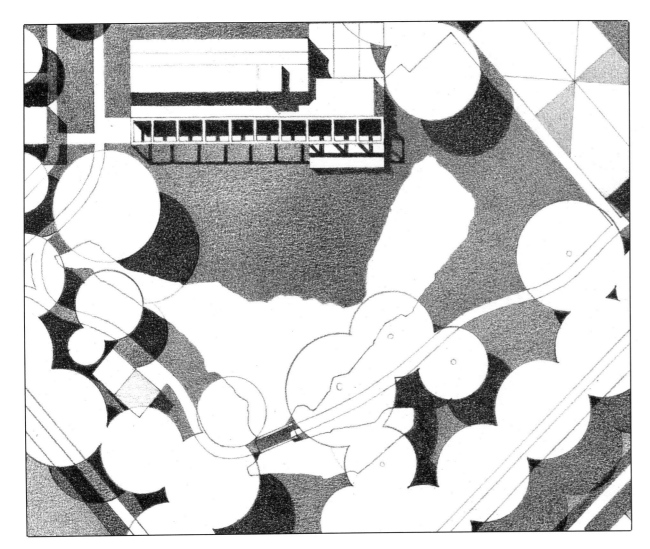

**Figure 4–6.**   *Time-saving, ground-revealing rendered abstraction of the site plan depicted in* Figure 4–4.

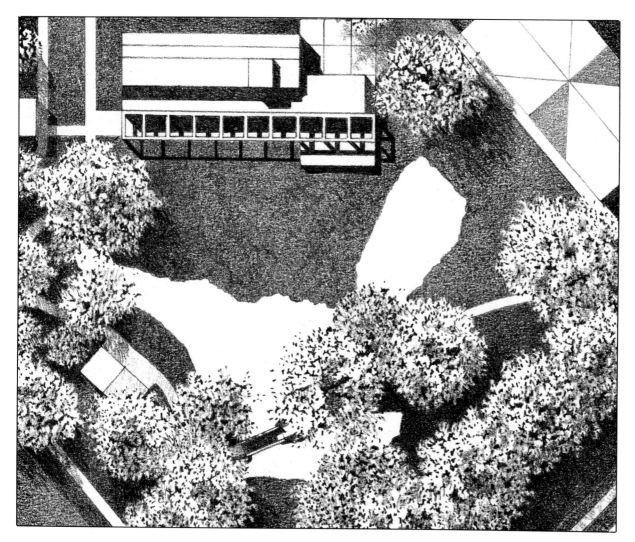

**Figure** 4–7. *Realistic, detailed interpretation of site plan in Figure 4–4.*

## Transparent Trees

A site plan, if rendered literally, may conceal beneath tree canopies certain important aspects of the design, such as the configuration of walkways and streets and the disposition of low-lying ground cover. In such cases, it is reasonable to make trees transparent or, in the extreme, to "section" selected trees, by rendering only their trunks.

## Mood

Mood in a site plan is created in several ways. One may darken the tonal key of the drawing in general, or depict dark and wildly growing trees, or include cloud shadows which streak diagonally across the entire site plan, affecting everything in their path. Mood is also enhanced by having the water appear choppy, suggesting the presence of wind. Occasionally, the sun's glare is seen on the surface of water. The plan view is sometimes depicted as if partially obscured by cloud cover, enhancing the feeling of actually looking down on the scene from an airplane. Mood may be either subtly interwoven into the theme of the drawing or applied sentimentally, like cake frosting, in overt attempts to strengthen the drawing's coherence.

## Selected Examples of the Plan View

The scale of the site plan affects the amount of detail included in our drawings. As the scale increases, we are forced to simplify form. The following pages illustrate site plans in increasing magnitudes of scale.

### Villa Julia

The plan view of Villa Julia, a mid-16th-century Italian villa, is illustrated in black and white on middle gray (Figure 4–8). Middle gray holds and defines the ground plane. White and black focus the viewer's attention on the most important aspect of the drawing, namely, the architectural elements arranged along the central visual axis of the composition. White is assumed to advance against gray. For this reason, the walls of the villa that are closer to the viewer than the ground plan are depicted in white.

Darker tones are used for shadows. These shadows not only lend a sense of depth to the drawing, they also reinforce the whiteness of the white areas through tonal contrast. The rendering has a stark, cold quality about it for the simple reason that its hard edges are not in contrast with the softer forms of natural landscape features like trees, water, and clouds.

### Villa Lante

As the scale of the site plan consumes larger parcels of the countryside, it becomes more difficult to show individual trees. This is evident in the plan view of Villa Lante, another Italian garden (Figure 4–9). In this example, individual trees are not indicated. Instead, delineation technique fuses the trees together into broad areas of texture.

### Elm Grove Park

This proposed park design for the Village of Elm Grove, Wisconsin, skillfully blends elements of English and French Renaissance garden art (Figure 4–10). As a rendering, it includes several techniques for making refined site plans. It is basically a black and white on middle gray tonal composition. The ground plane is rendered in subtle variations of middle gray, with important features of the landscape such as buildings and trees indicated in white or off-white. The plan includes various kinds of tree groupings. Some of the trees are organized in rows. Their individual outlines blend together to strengthen the overall pattern of their linear arrangement. Other trees are organized into casual groupings. Some trees overlap, others touch, still others clump together.

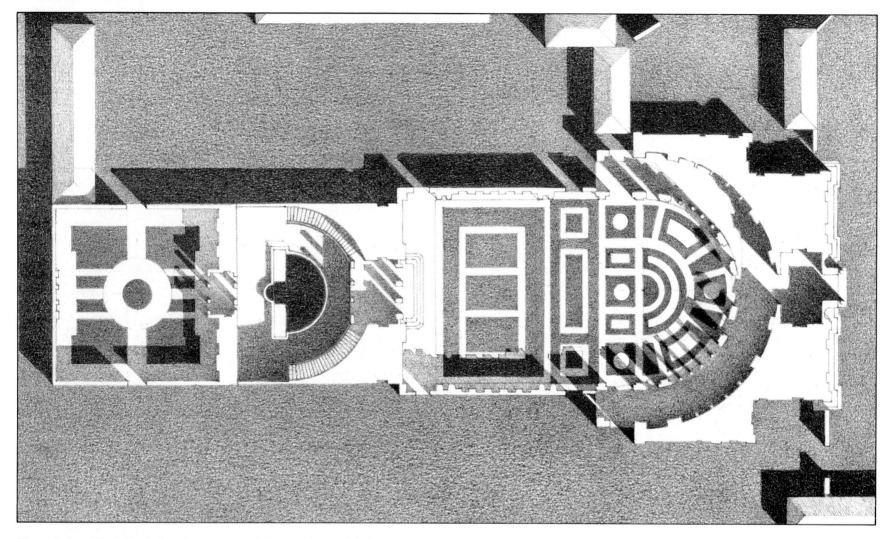

**Figure 4–8.**    Villa Julia: *A clean-shaven gray ground plane provides a stark backdrop for this 16th-century Italian villa.*

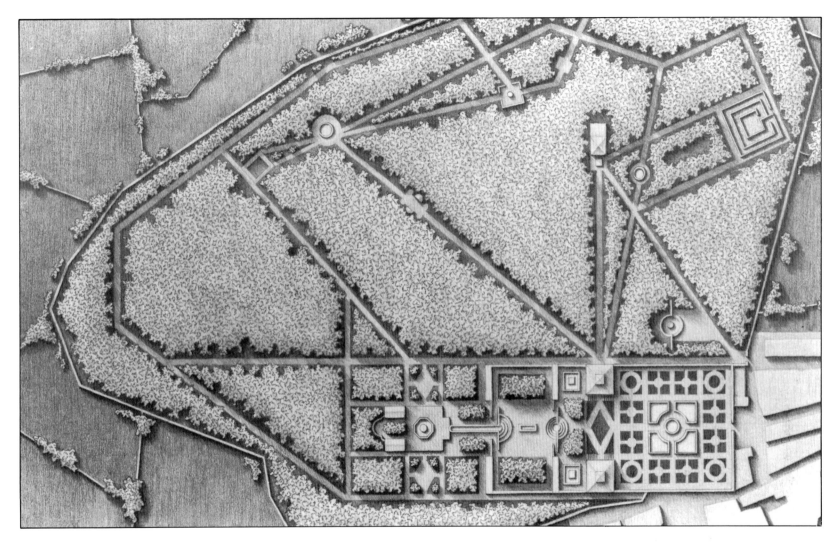

*Figure 4–9.* Villa Lante: *Greater altitudes fuse groups of trees into thicket-like single units outlined by man-made paths and ways.*

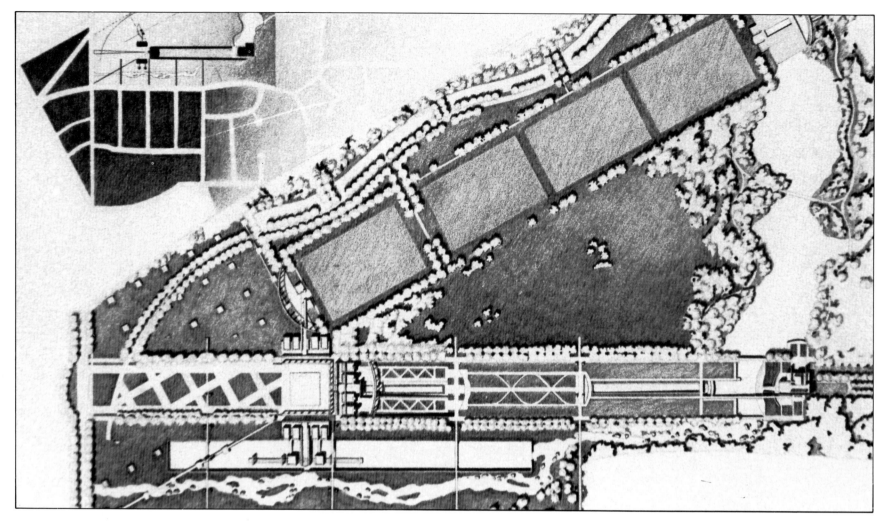

**Figure 4–10.** Elm Grove Park proposal: *A skillful blend of different historic styles and graphic techniques is evident in this site plan.*

# Chapter 5

# Magnified Contexts

*But, after all, the only principle in art is to copy what you see. Dealers in aesthetics to the contrary, every other method is fatal. There is no recipe for improving nature. The only thing is to see.*

AUGUSTE RODIN

*But this blade of grass leads him to study every plant and then the seasons, the wide aspects of the countryside, then animals, then the human figure. So he passes his life, and life is too short to do the whole . . .*

VINCENT VAN GOGH

*To say to the painter, that Nature is to be taken as she is, is to say to the player, that he may sit on the piano.*

JAMES WHISTLER

A tree, bathed in light, casts the shadow of its branches on leaves that lay on the ground. This ground, in turn, recedes to the horizon where it joins the sky. The totality of these interconnected parts describes one overall visual scene.

It's easy to take our visual surroundings for granted. Normally, we notice neither the dishpan nor the sunset as we navigate our way through a world that lies somewhere in between the mundane and the spectacular. This chapter urges the reader to appreciate the nuances of our daily lives so that a wider range of everyday sensations may be articulated in our renderings. To aid in developing a heightened awareness of surroundings, this chapter advocates rendering trees and other landscape features as they appear in context, not as isolated phenomena.

Visual context can be thought of in two basic ways. One way freezes movement in order to study scale, the other freezes scale to study movement. Gordon Cullen, an outspoken advocate of the latter method of analysis, preferred to hold spatial scale constant so that he could examine bodily movement through environments. In his classic book, *The Concise Townscape*, Cullen advocated sketching places in sequence. He felt that in getting to where we wanted to go, the scene as it unfolded through time was important. He wondered: what is it like, in six perspectives or less, to stroll through quaint little villages or public parks? To create these sequences, Cullen kept the focal distance on his mental camera constant. He did not zoom in and out on subject matter.

The approach toward the analysis of pictorial imagery presented in this chapter is in many respects the opposite of Cullen's approach. This is based solely on the idea of scale magnification. Sequences are frozen in time so that they can be studied in terms of changing scale. The visual world is bracketed between the extremes of near and far. To facilitate this particular approach, context is divided into six stepped magnifications: ground plane, building wall, interior room, exterior place, vista, and prospect.

These categories could further be subdivided or reduced in number, but that's not the issue. It's the idea of scale progression that's important here. By studying a series of drawings organized in scale progression, the renderer is forced to accept the gradual loss of objectivity that accompanies contexts depicted at increasing magnitudes of size.

The idea of a scale progression can be expressed in various ways. For example, a progression can be assembled with images collected from different settings. The first drawing in a series of magnified contexts might depict rocks on a beach, and the last drawing, a desert highway. On the other hand, scale progressions may consist of images gathered from the same setting.

The Marietta House in Milwaukee, Wisconsin (Figure 5–1) is the subject of three of the renderings that make up the progression of six magnified contexts in this chapter. Figure 5–4 depicts an exterior wall of Marietta House. Figure 5–6 depicts the view of an interior room, Figure 5–10 illustrates a view of Marietta House from across the street.

## Working From Photographs

Sketching from nature is an important exercise in learning how to draw. While useful, it nonetheless must be admitted that in many situations it hinders our ability to really see in detail what it is that we are looking at. Trees sway in the breeze. Clouds move gently across our view. Shadows creep slowly over buildings. To overcome this problem, in some situations, I have found the meticulous study of landscape contexts is made more effective if I work from pictures. Like a mother pleading with child to hold still for the camera, the artist working directly from nature becomes very frustrated when, for example, a moving van parks directly in the middle of the scene. Pictures hold context still, and freeze it in its tracks. Thus frozen, images can be scrupulously examined for subtlety. We have time to decide on the best way to capture the sense of spatial depth in our drawings. We can experiment with different line strokes for molding the shapes of things.

While we most certainly gain valuable insight into the subtleties of pictorial depiction when we copy or trace from photographs, it is not without sacrifice. For example, in tracing, we cannot develop skill at capturing proportion and contour. This must be learned elsewhere. In addition, working from photographs also removes from the drawing process the multidimensional feelings that we experience when we sketch in real settings: the touch of the furniture, the sound of the water, the temperature and humidity of the breeze; the subtle and peculiar odors in the air. When we sketch out of doors, we are saturated in nature, alive and breathing. The calm and silence of the distance is more deeply felt in opposition to the sensory congestion of the foreground.

Obviously, remaining indoors and copying or tracing from photographs is quite different from being in the scene as we render. Good draw-

**Figure 5–1.** *The artist's hand gives a brick building an adobe appearance and transforms ordinary shrubbery into luminous foliage. Uncurtained windows appear dark and empty, as if this noble-looking house is occupied but nobody is home.*

**Figure 5–2.** *Cracked, broken concrete and splintered wood, blades of grass, twigs, husks, and patches of pebbles mingle in a confused and close entanglement. Such detail can leave grass stains on the observer's nose.*

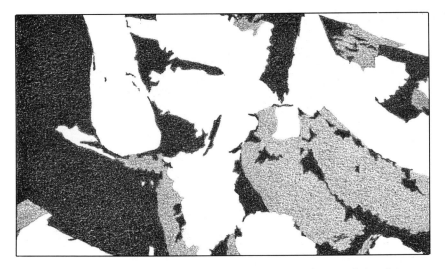

*Figure 5–3.* *Diagram: Omitting details, patterns of light and dark contrast become obvious.*

ings, however, can be made from photographs of places visited in reality. The memories of such places can be stored and recalled during the delineation process. We must experience the depicted scene firsthand in order to have a true sense of it. Without this experience, we risk a diluted interpretation of the raw visual data contained in the photograph.

## Ground Plane

Diverse textural features seem to sprout like weeds from a very thin soil (Figure 5–2). Literal realism of the sort illustrated in this figure is evident at this viewing distance because there is little spatial dimension to the picture and therefore no need to address the problem of depth of field. All of our energies can be focused on the singular problem of capturing every last nuance of texture and form.

Figure 5–2 was traced from a photograph. It was traced in layers, about ten in all. The first layer captured the drawing's pure blacks and whites. Successive layers slowly built upon the first toward the rendering's final full range of tonal values (Figure 5–3). It is worth mentioning here that if the drawing had been copied from a photograph rather than traced, the rendering process would have been reversed. That is, the first layer would have been very light and successive layers would have built up toward darker values to the final full tonal range.

Note that the pencil strokes defining each blade of grass seem to heighten each blade's three-dimensional appearance. This could only be achieved because the delineator was willing to take the time to visualize actual conditions of texture, shadow, and overlap for each individual feature in the photograph. Observe the subtle buildup of the pencil strokes that define the concrete. Compare the pencil technique for rendering the surfaces smoothed by a mason's trowel with the jaggedness of the broken edges, which is expressed through an intricate play of light and shadow.

Rendering with an eye for photographic realism requires patience. In

**Figure 5–4.** *A young man seated at a drafting table is barely visible through the dark reflections of nearby trees on canted panes of glass.*

*Figure 5–5.* *Diagram: Deliberate omission of detail reveals contrast pattern.*

addition, the care with which every detail is rendered must complement the drawing's sense of overall tonal composition and balance. It is easy to depict details while losing sight of the composition of the whole. The difficulty is in bringing detail and composition together into a single totality.

Figure 5–2 is in sharp focus across its entire field. Emphasis on the shoes is provided primarily through strong tonal light/dark contrast. This emphasis is further enhanced through tonal contrasts in texture and detail. The drawing, executed in black Prismacolor pencil, required approximately five days to complete.

## Building Wall

Close inspection of any building wall reveals a hidden world of intricate spatial corners, peculiar details, and unexpected juxtapositions of materials. Old and crooked walls curtained with decayed mortar joints and dented aluminum downspouts, with weeds sprouting from every orifice, are interesting to look at. So are walls painted with signs or laminated with posters—Gas for Less, Muffler Repair, Roommate Wanted, Typist for hire, etc. There are windows in walls and windowed walls. Windows are frustrating to illustrate. It is not easy to balance the transparency and reflectivity of glass.

Every building wall has its ambiguous viewing distance, meaning the distance from which, on the one hand, details are too small and numerous to render with precision, and, on the other hand, too large to abstract. One way to compensate for the extra amount of time required to render details at ambiguous viewing distances is to focus the rendering.

Focus was achieved in Figure 5–4 by concentrating contrasts of tone and detail toward the center of the drawing. For the most part, the level of detail in the drawing is the strongest and sharpest in the area of this focus. As indicated in Figure 5–5, the tonal focus is centered on the French door. The door's grid of muntins—the vertical and horizontal sticks that hold its glass panes in place—were made white in order to contrast with a dark background. Contrast is strongest for those muntins framing the shadowy figure sitting at his desk. Because the eye glides easily over areas of constant tonal value and changing texture, the many diverse shapes and textures within the outlined area of the rendering seem to visually cohere.

**Figure 5–6.** *Windows are pictures of daylight on otherwise dark walls. Indoors, natural and artificial lighting take sides in a battle of surface illumination.*

*Figure* 5–7.  *Lighting diagram: Tonal contrasts are balanced in detail's absence.*

## Interior Room

On a bright and sunny day, the lighting level outdoors is as much as 1,000 times greater than indoors. Because of the extreme imbalance of this contrast ratio, light from outside streams into rooms, not the other way around (Figure 5–6). A simple squint of the eye while looking toward a real window confirms this condition. The squinted impression of an interior window is reduced to a blurred image of a bright opening silhouetted against dark interior walls and surfaces.

Interior windows are as luminous as the light pouring in through them. In a rendering, however, the brightness of an interior window is dictated by the paper. To heighten the feeling of sunlit windows, experience delineators often darken the tonal value of the surfaces surrounding window openings. The walls around a window, even if intrinsically white, are often depicted at 50 percent gray or more in order to create a sense of very bright light from outside.

To further enhance this feeling, the renderer can use other devices as well, such as glare, light fringe, and light stream.

Silhouette, glare, and fringe are illustrated in Figure 5–7. In this figure, the window on the right is in silhouette: only a dark outline of the window muntins stands out against the light background. The effect of glare is evident in the washed-out vertical window mullions toward the center of the left window. The tonal contrast between light source and its surrounding is so strong, a kind of hazy white appears around the light source. This effect can be seen by staring into the headlights of oncoming cars with their brights on. Fringe lighting occurs around the head of the figure seated at the drafting table. It involves a bleaching out of the profile of rounded forms under intense lighting.

Not illustrated here is the effect of light stream. Bands of light appear to streak onto smoke-filled rooms through windows. Each streak of light lightens the tonal value of the features it overlaps. As a rule-of-thumb, we may lighten the tonal value of features in the path of light streaks by a factor of half the measure between the surfaces' intrinsic value and white.

**Figure** 5–8.    *Reclined in a white metal lawn chair, hot feet wrapped in dirty tennis shoes and propped upon a tractor tire, the artist sizes subject matter for his sketch. Watery light washes away distant details.*

***Figure* 5—9.** *Diagram: Tonal contrasts provide basis for balance in depth and breadth of pictorial space.*

## Exterior Place

It was late afternoon. The tractor had just finished digging a trench for the driveway. The kids in the neighborhood had gone home for dinner. Don fetched a lawn chair and began sketching the house across the street (Figure 5—8).

Jumbled outdoor landscape scenery, visual flea markets of assorted trees and shrubbery, are easy to render, but only if three attributes of the rendering are coordinated at once. These attributes include: (1) level of detail; (2) overall spatial organization; and (3) compositional focus.

The scene in Figure 5—8 is rendered in atmospheric perspective. There are fewer details further in the background. Sharp, crisp edges and corners dominate the foreground, where the shadows and reflections on the shiny metal surfaces of the tractor contrast with the less specific treatment of surfaces of the house across the street. Individual bricks on the house in the distance are not visible, only the generalized tonal value of brick walls.

Other renderings devices are included. The foreground is sunny, so silhouettes of the tractor, the head, hand, and feet are kept light and white, tonally detached from the grayed elements in the midground. The person's hand, especially around the thumb, is blurred, its outline somewhat indistinct due to the harsh, direct sunlight on its rounded form.

The rendering's focus is targeted on the house's porch across the street. Strong tonal contrast was used to heighten this focus (Figure 5—9). The trunk of the tree toward the right center of the drawing frames this focus.

The subtle yet visible underlying textural constancy of the paper's grain was another attribute of the drawing taken into consideration. The rendering, in spite of its visual complexity, nonetheless holds together partly because of the uniform leaking through of the paper's texture across the entire breadth of the composition.

**Figure 5–10.**    *The street's vista emerges from a dull gray background into a leafy confusion of disorder in the foreground.*

*Figure 5–11.* *Diagram: Vista and focal point balance in this tonal diagram.*

## Vista

A vista is a view with tunnel vision, a controlled outlook. More precisely, a vista is what anybody sees viewing the length of anything long, straight, and narrow. The corridors and hallways of dormitories and hotels as well as the runways of airports form vistas.

The skewed view of a residential street is depicted in Figure 5–10. In this scene, the vista itself doesn't dominate as forcefully as does the Italian garden vista illustrated in Figure 6–4. Perhaps it is because the terminus of the vista illustrated here is not located dead center in the composition. Or maybe it is because the leaf canopies of the shapeless scruffy trees along Marietta Avenue are just too ragged to suggest the visual walls of a tunnel.

If the viewer of the scene sees the double track of this ragged tree-lined corridor only out of the corner of one eye, it is because competing with it is yet another focus, that of the carport just to the right of center. It is here that the strongest tonal contrasts and sharpest details dwell (Figure 5–11). Two foci battle for attention. The strong, clean details, hard-edged geometries, and sharp tonality of the architectural carport competes with the softer, looser naturalistic forms of trees and other landscape features that make up the vista on the left side of the rendering. The carport wins, because the rough, vertical line strokes on the left side of the rendering lack definition and sharpness. This weak application of graphite dilutes visual impact.

## Prospect

The French called them "coulisses," meaning "wings of a theater." They are the vertical features arranged at the sides of a picture in order to direct the viewer's eye toward a focus. In Figure 5–12, a pictorial framing device in the form of a massive tree is situated in the foreground of the rendering.

In this rendering, the tree works effectively as a framing device for three reasons. First, it engages the viewer by bringing cozy, familiar imagery associated with the tactile feel of gnarled bark to within arm's reach. Second, the tree mediates the gap in depth between the viewer and the rendering's distant background scenery. Third, the tree frames the view, directing the viewer's eye into the picture toward its chief point of interest.

For the sake of convenience, features in perspective are often divided into foreground, midground, and background. In reality, we know that foreground and background are not separated. We know that the dirt beneath our feet extends in one shape or another to the horizon in the distance. Yet, we tend to instinctively divide the features of the rendering into depth zones. The word "tree," for example, suggests a midground shape. "Trunk" and "bark" are the ingredients of its foreground appearance

and "woodland" describes a background feature which itself is composed of trees. Window, building, skyline suggest another kind of mental word progression into depth. In Figure 5–12, the pictorial space consists of three depth zones. There is a dark frontal foreground plane, made up of tree trunk and leafy matter; a light watery horizontal midground plane; and a medium-gray wooded background plane. During the rendering process, the tonal values of each of these three depth zones was deliberately exaggerated. The foreground is dark though textured with flecks of light; the midground is generally very light; and the background is middle-gray.

Perspective tends to invert hierarchies of scale and significance. That is to say, in perspective, nothing is truly small. The most powerful and important feature of a depicted scene, the massive mountain, the towering skyscraper, the mile-long bridge, can be dwarfed in the perspective view by the most trivial foreground feature, a rubber waste basket, an old broom handle, a kitchen cabinet door. As a result, the amount of time required to depict various features in a perspective is often inversely related to their significance. The bark on the foreground tree in Figure 5–12 required the most time to render because of the intricacy of its many overlaying textures, tones, and patterns. The band of trees on the other side of the lake required the least time to delineate.

**Figure** 5–12.    *Vivid foreground greenery darts in short, abrupt zigzags against the backdrop of
a lake buffed by a sluggish breeze.*

# Chapter 6

# The Unfolding Landscape

*The order observed in painting a landscape . . . is as follows: First, one draws it, dividing it into three or four distances or planes. In the foremost, where one places the figure or saint, one draws the largest trees and rocks, proportionate to the scale of the figure. In the second, smaller trees and houses are drawn; in the third yet smaller, and in the fourth, where the mountain ridges meet the sky, one ends with the greatest diminution of all.*

FRANCISCO PACHECO

*The whole of nature is metaphor of the human mind.*

RALPH WALDO EMERSON

*That Nature is always right, is an assertion, artistically, as untrue, as it is one whose truth is universally taken for granted. Nature is very rarely right, to such an extent even, that it might almost be said that Nature is usually wrong; that is to say, the condition of things that shall bring about the perfection of harmony worthy a picture is rare, and not common at all.*

JAMES WHISTLER

It is one thing to depict a leaf, a twig, or a tree. It is yet another to portray a carpet of crabgrass or an orchard of fruit trees in the rolling green valley of a broad landscape.

As the rendered landscape expands to include deeper and broader interpretations of pictorial depth, alternative methods for depicting its unfolding features must be explored. Pictorial scenes that include both near and far phenomena strain the renderer's ability to portray all features, large and small, in the same literal way.

If there is a key to rendering full and beautiful landscapes, it is this: natural landscapes unfold. Examples of organic forms that unfold are everywhere around us. Flowers bloom. Water from the nozzle of a garden hose dissipates from jet stream to sparkling spray. Popcorn explodes from kernel to puff.

Just as organic forms unfold, so do less tangible phenomena. The eye itself zooms in and out of settings. Even as I sit at the kitchen table for breakfast, the whole of the scene before my eyes unfolds: I stare at the pulp ring in my orange juice glass. From there, my gaze shifts to the linoleum floor, then over to the steaming, clanking radiator in the corner. My gaze wanders to the window. Through the faint reflection of a ceiling fixture in the window glass, I see an apartment building silhouetted against neon streaks of low-flying clouds tinted pink-orange by the glow of the city's sodium-vapor street lights.

This chapter looks at the unfolding process from the standpoint of historic landscape gardens. It organizes these gardens into a series of four specific images: the room, the vista, the prospect, and the view. Each

**Figure 6–1.**    *Sunken parterre in the Queen's Garden, the Royal Botanic Gardens, Kew Palace, London.*

*Figure 6–2.    Diagram: Spatial layering through alternating bands of tonal contrast.*

successive formal garden space captures a deeper, broader, and less tangible kind of pictorial experience. The four spaces are represented by the Medieval room, the 16th-century Italian vista, the 17th-century French prospect, and the 18th-century English view.

## The Medieval Room

Long ago, the word "garden" meant enclosure. The word "paradise" (in old Persian, "pairideza") also meant enclosure. The medieval conception of the pleasure garden, a place enclosed, reflected people's need for refuge from a savage wilderness.

The Queen's Garden behind Kew Palace in England is laid out in the manner of an English medieval garden (Figure 6–1). The view here places the spectator in the middle of an outdoor room, in a sunken parterre, looking toward a pleached archway that is just beyond a tall, dark wall of clipped greenery. There is a small reflecting pool straight ahead. From where we stand as we look at this pool, our viewing angle of the still water's surface is maybe 15 degrees above horizontal. Because of this acute viewing angle, the water in the pool behaves more like a mirror than a window to the pool's bottom. Reflections of the perimeter stone basin are therefore visible in the water's surface as is the reflection of the statue's pedestal in the center of the pool.

The rendering's pictorial space is layered. The tall hedge defines the room's principle spatial boundary and is therefore rendered very darkly. Figure 6–2 indicates the tonal strength of each of the drawing's multiple frontal planes. The sense of spatial depth is based primarily on subtle overlapping of frontal planes. Very little depth is indicated by tonal gradation. The flat tonal frontal planes are visually separated from each other by horizontal surfaces exposed to sunlight. The tonal focus is centered on the pool in the middle. The monotony of the tall dark hedge and the overall symmetry of the space is broken by the white statue toward the right.

In terms of pencil technique, the water in the pool was illustrated with simple horizontal lines. The shimmering, transparent quality of pleached archway and background trees was achieved by using a very sharp pencil point. Pencil marks were spaced so as to leave traces of white paper between each line.

*Figure 6–3.* *Cypress Alley, Boboli Garden, Florence, Italy.*

*Figure 6–4.* *Diagram: A tossed salad of tonal planes is held together by the rendering's strong central visual axis.*

## The Italian Vista

The Cypress Alley in the Boboli Garden, Florence, Italy, was laid out in 1550 by Tribolo and Buontalenti. Viewed from its summit, this tunnel-like alley is varied, lush, and resplendent with leafy contrasts (Figure 6–3).

At the foot of its incline, framed by the green alley walls, is a round island contained within an oval basin. The island has a fountain in its center.

The vista here is axial, like a city street. The view, which terminates on the fountain in the midground, is channeled by the green wall of trees and other landscape features on either side of the alley. Because of our commanding position near the hill's summit, our eye is able to easily wander over the top of the formal alley, taking in the panorama of the distant surrounding countryside.

The space, although channeled and focused, is nonetheless heavily layered. As indicated in Figure 6–4, foreground trees silhouette against indistinct and hazy background features. In the distance, the space is not so distinctly layered. Foreground merges into midground which in turn blends into background. The generalized movement of the eye into the depths of the pictorial field is continuously interrupted by the dissonant array of features that define this movement.

The sense of depth in this rendering was enhanced through the use of atmospheric perspective. Contrasting tones and textures in sharp detail animate the foreground. Flat tones, texture, and detail define the background.

Textures vary considerably in the Italian landscape. Trees are gnarled and twisted, some looking like picked chicken bones. In the rendering, variety of texture does not disintegrate into visual chaos because features are grouped tonally according to their depth in the pictorial space. The eye glides easily over areas of changing texture and constant tone.

The tonal prominence of the entry gate to the isolotta at the base of the hill serves to frame the avenue's terminus, the fountain of Oceanus. White flecks of raw paper are visible in the texture of the clipped hedges in the extreme foreground. High tonal contrast was used as a device to bring the hedges perceptually closer to the viewer.

*Figure 6–5.*    *Formal garden at Vaux le Vicomte, near Melon, France.*

***Figure 6–6.*** *Diagram of measured recession into pictorial space.*

## The French Prospect

The view cuts diagonally across the main axis of Vaux le Vicomte, the famous French chateau and garden (Figure 6–5). Designed during the 17th century by André LeNotre, this elaborate formal garden behind the chateau at Vaux le Vicomte is considered by many the finest, purest example of French Renaissance garden art.

In spite of the open feel of this garden, it is in fact visually enclosed. Movement into depth terminates at the crest of the gentle slope of the distant hill, on a false horizon. In this regard, LeNotre's intention was to position people who visited the garden in the middle of a very large bowl of space, with the bowl's rim symbolizing the horizon.

We can gauge the size of this garden on the basis of the spacing of its topiary—the many dark, clipped conical tree massings that punctuate the garden's ground plane. The calculated, measured, stepped recession of topiary into the background stands in counterpoint with the smooth, serene recession of the garden's grassy carpet.

Visual movement into the most distant reaches of the garden is interrupted by the sunken water canal that cuts laterally across the garden's primary visual axis. The spectator must actually walk around this canal in order to reach the summit of the hill in the far distance.

The rendering in Figure 6–5 relies heavily on the effects of atmospheric perspective. The recession of topiary in the foreground parterres was handled carefully, lest the technique for delineating textures disrupts the sense of progression into space. The rendering's composition is divided in half by the major diagonal movement of topiary. Above this dark diagonal band of clipped trees, the drawing recedes through progressively diminishing alternating horizontal bands of tonal contrast (Figure 6–6). The background is treated in flat tones. Pencil strokes were spaced just far enough apart to provide a shimmering effect.

*Figure* 6–7.   *Garden at Stourhead in Wiltshire, England.*

*Figure 6–8.* *Diagram: Tonal description of rendering's overall spatial configuration.*

## The English View

The view of lake with bridge is located on the grounds of Stourhead Garden in Wiltshire, England (Figure 6–7). The garden, which was designed and laid out by its owner, Henry Hoare, in the mid-18th century, remains to this today a celebration of the English landscaping dictum: all of nature is a garden. The scene depicted here does not rely upon the straight-line geometries of hard-edged walls for its sense of enclosure, but rather achieves its expansive spatial shape through the less obtrusive placement of natural landscape features themselves.

The rendering's simplified overall pictorial space is filled with abrupt, irregular contrasts of tone and texture. The view includes an open foreground, like a stage platform. The foreground trees on the left side of the picture are balanced in the composition by at least two other features that double-function as markers in guiding the eye into every deeper regions of the pictorial space. The effects of atmospheric perspective are evident in the rendering. Depth was assumed to filter out contrasts of tone, texture, and detail hierarchically. Contrasts of tone and texture are stronger in the foreground than the background. The rendering's basic spatial configuration is expressed in Figure 6–8.

The lake splits the rendering in half horizontally. It is worth noting that the perimeter of this lake is not round like a circle. Its shape in plan view more closely resembles the three-fingered star created by three touching circles of the same diameter. A lake shaped in this way achieves greater horizontal visual extension within a single eye-level perspective view than a lake in the shape of a circle. It may seem to extend around corners.

On the other side of the lake is a miniature Pantheon. Nestled amidst the trees like an egg in a bird's nest, it invites the viewer to visit it. But the path to the Pantheon is not as the crow flies. Rather, the visitor must travel a circuitous route by foot along the lake's edge. Obviously, eye and foot are not in agreement here. The garden's designer deliberately exploited this contrast.

For stability, the visual weight of the darker tones of the rendering were concentrated toward the bottom of the composition. The Turf bridge was made a strong focal point in the composition by emphasizing its dark silhouette against the water. To prevent the bridge from floating as an object, both ends were linked to the ground plane. Trees in the background were rendered in a nearly constant tone of moderately varying texture.

# Chapter 7

# The Illusion Becomes Real

*A painting will be elegant when the extreme distances are connected to the foregrounds by means of the middle distances in such a way that they will contrast neither too feebly nor with too much harshness of lines and colors.*

NICOLAS POUSSIN

*When you shall have acquired some proficiency in foreground material, your next step should be the study of atmosphere—the power which defines and measures space.*

ASHER DURAND

*People who try to explain pictures are usually barking up the wrong tree.*

PABLO PICASSO

Aspiring renderers often struggle with the idea of copying, intimidated by a fear that the pencil-rendered duplicate is unimaginative. More than likely, this mental block is due to some silent inner voice of the artist which tells him to reject the copy as plagiarism, to reject it as nothing more than an underhanded, counterfeit, a loathsome fraud. It is with this same attitude that many rendering and sketching books tend to avoid discussion of both copying and tracing.

This book accepts entirely the benefits and advantages of copying as a direct means to an impressive end. The concern here is not whether a picture is an original or a duplicate, but rather whether the renderer has an understanding of spatial relationships suggested in the rendering.

Granted, copying from photographs or drawings is useless as an exercise if the copy is merely a dim, rubber-stamp impression of the original. To learn from the copying exercise, the renderer must be willing to interpret the original picture by digging beneath its surface, mentally carving out the terrain of its spatial subject matter. The renderer who can grasp spatial order in this way is intellectually equipped to locate new features in a scene, and to shift features and illumination as well.

## The Renderer's Total Visual Field

It is an oversimplification to assume that every detail within any given scene is grasped and portrayed by the renderer on the same level of abstraction. The experienced renderer's interpretation of subject matter varies depending upon the scale of the space to be depicted and the distance of particular features from the eye of the spectator. In the case of classical landscape painting, the diminishing detail that accompanied increasing pictorial depth was handled by partitioning the picture's visual field into three zonal distances: near, middle, and far. The same words for expressing the division of large-scale pictorial space are adopted here. Three pictorial zones, near, middle, and far, constitute what this book refers to as rendered realism's total visual field. In this chapter, we will assume that the near is associated with objective interpretations of subject matter, the middle distance with pictorial or perceptual interpretations, and the far with optical or conceptual interpretations.

There are advantages to interpreting pictorial content according to these three zones. The illustrator who grasps the nuances of rendering's total visual field can "push" features back or "pull" them forward into pictorial space in order to achieve balance in depth. In addition, a basic understanding of the zonal qualities of the total pictorial field allows the renderer to generate scenes that did not previously exist.

## Modelling the Total Visual Field

The clearest way for me to explain to another person how I visualize various features within the pictorial space of my renderings is to build physical models of my spatial interpretations of rendered scenes. With these models, other people can directly see how I perceive rendered space.

The type of physical model that demonstrates how I interpret rendered space does not look like a normal architectural model. It looks more like a miniature stage set. In general, this stage set consists of not one but three different kinds of spaces. One space is objective, another is pictorial, and the other is optical (Figure 7–1). Many of the renderings in this book were developed in terms of these three spatial categories. In the process of rendering Figure 9–17, for example, every leaf of the plant in the foreground was portrayed objectively. The sunroom was depicted pictorially, in perspective; and the background was interpreted optically, as a flat surface.

"I therefore wished to compose pictures on canvas similar to representations on the stage; and farther hope that they will be tried by the same test, and criticized by the same criterion," wrote William Hogarth in 1793.

"Ocular demonstration would carry more conviction to the mind of the sensible man, than all he would find in a thousand volumes."

Stage sets mimic how a scene is perceived and ordered in the mind of the renderer. In fact, the stage set designer and the renderer think alike in matters regarding the features that make up realism's total visual field. The renderer interprets features in the pictorial space as if they are stage sets. The stage set designer constructs stage sets so that they can be viewed as renderings.

## Theatrical Realism

In the third chapter of Sebastiano Serlio's *Second Booke*, published in 1545, is a short folio entitled: *A Treatise of Scenes, or places to play in*. This section of Serlio's book includes detailed illustrations on how to make comic, tragic, and satirical theatrical scenery. What makes these stage sets notable is their very realistic depth of spatial field. That is, from the vantage point of a person seated in the audience, the space of the stage looks much deeper than it actually is. Inigo Jones' 17th-century stage sets were patterned after Serlio's. They consisted of: (1) a proscenium arch; (2) side wings with a raked stage; (3) a scene of relief; and (4) a backdrop.

As illustrated in Figure 7–1, the procenium arch was the frame that separated the stage proper from the stage apron and audience. Side wings were the tall, L-shaped panels that stepped back on both sides of the stage. The floor of the raked stage sloped gently upward toward the back of the stage. The scene of relief consisted of one or more layers of painted panels with cutouts. The backdrop was a large painting that closed off the back of the stage.

Today's theatrical realism has not changed much since Serlio's time. The stage recedes from the audience into a back wall. The stage front is framed by the proscenium. Scenery on stage is painted or constructed in perspective. The effect is that of an interior room or an outdoor space.

In the theater of realism, with its simple staging devices, whole pictorial scenes are portrayed. Furthermore, because scenes are modelled in the third dimension, it is possible to change the appearance of the stage set by varying its illumination effects.

# Objective, Pictorial, and Optical Interpretations of the Total Visual Field

The renderer's total visual field consists of every conceivable arrangement of particular features that can be imagined in a realistic scene. Here, we shall assume that the total visual field is divided, like the theater of realism's stage, into three types of space, i.e., objective, pictorial, and optical, which correspond to near, middle, and far zonal distances, respectively (Figure 7–1). These three distinct types of spaces represent three ways of interpreting the features in a rendered scene.

## Objective Space

*That painting is the most praiseworthy is most like the thing represented.*

LEONARDO DA VINCI

The tactile, audible elements on the theater of realism's stage—its actors, horses, and furniture—exist in the theater's objective space.

In a rendering, subject matter understood in a literal, objective way is interpreted as if in objective space. Features in objective space can be shifted around like stage props without changing their size or shape.

## Pictorial Space

*. . . and Raphael Durbin, was not he a most cunning Paynter, and an excellent Perspective Artist, before he became an Architector?*

SEBASTIANO SERLIO

In the theater of realism, the middle space of the stage, molded as it is by side wings and raked stage, resides in pictorial space.

In a rendering, pictorial space itself plays a role in shaping the features in the middle distance of the depicted scene. The dimension of depth is attenuated, foreshortened.

## Optical Space

*For me a picture is a plane surface covered with representations of objects . . .*

MARK CHAGALL

On the stage, some visual imagery is not modelled three-dimensionally. Rather, in order to save time and expense, it is painted to look three-dimensional on the flat surfaces of stage wings and backdrops. In other words, while the image on the stage wing or backdrop may appear three-dimensional, the backdrop itself is one-dimensional.

The illustrator may group related features in the rendering into layers of flat, frontal depth planes. Distant skylines and mountains are often interpreted "in the flat."

*Figure 7–1.* Inigo Jones' stage sets consisted of (1) proscenium arch; (2) side wings with raked stage; (3) scene of relief; and (4) backdrop. This model includes objective, pictorial, and optical interpretations of space.

## Eight Spatial Modes

The rendering's near, middle, and far distances can be further subdivided to include eight spatial interpretations:

1. Literal objects with names—renderings of three-dimensional things, like people, trees, cars, buildings, with no evidence of the background or setting;
2. Finite volumetric spaces—renderings of rooms with walls.
3. Perspective space—renderings that conform to the principles of linear perspective;
4. Gravitational space—renderings that take into account the influence of gravity in shaping the features in the pictorial field;
5. Atmospheric space—renderings that include atmospheric or luminous spatial effects.
6. Layered space—renderings that separate features into distinct layered cut-out planes. Silhouette effects fall under this heading;
7. Masked space—renderings that divide the picture itself into areas of transparency and opacity. For example, a painting divided into luminous back-lit sky and opaque earth;
8. Screened space—renderings understood completely in the plane, like a photograph or painted scenic backdrop.

## The Objective Interpretation

Objective realism emphasizes the depiction of a material thing in hand, not the perceptual experience of the thing at a distance (Figures 7–2, 7–3).

Objective space is the stuff of common everyday experience. In terms of theatrical realism, the actors and their props, that is, the actual sofas and chairs they sit in or throw about, exist in objective space. Because the space is objective, the actor moving around on the stage does not undergo Alice in Wonderland distortional changes in size and shape due to the effects of the surrounding space. Objects can be illuminated from all angles with no distortion of shade and shadow effects.

In terms of rendering, the near-depth zone of objective space is capable of describing objects in hyper-realistic, explicit, vivid detail.

Objects, in their most literal sense, have strong visual character. They tend to stand out in the rendering because they are expressed in such vivid detail. We can identify the materials of which they are made, like wood grain, shiny metal, and soft feathers and fur.

Objective things like toasters and coffee mugs have finite, self-contained, particular forms. They have strong centers of gravity. Unlike the sky or a mountain range, objective things are comparatively small and portable. We feel as if we can touch them or wrap our arms around them. At the very least, we feel as if we can walk around them.

Several of the renderings in this book include close-up depictions of hands. In each case, the hand is the nearest feature in the rendering, deliberately pushed toward a literal, objective interpretation. Pencil strokes conform to the rounded contours of the skin. Knuckle hairs, blemishes and freckles may be evident. Strong tonal contrasts and explicit detail contribute to the literal, objective interpretation.

Objective forms exist in volumetric spatial surroundings. Volumetric spaces and objective forms are inseparable. Objective forms are contained in volumetric space; volumetric space is shaped by objective form. We understand volumetric space through the objective forms that give it definition.

## Literal Objects With Names

Rendering with the idea to capture realistically an object involves drawing only the object, not the space surrounding the object. Pencil doodles, close-up depictions of kitchen appliances, and quick design sketches of furniture pieces are all examples of drawings in which the object appears to float in a contextural void.

We interpret the intentions of the artist who illustrates floating objects in one of two ways. Either the artist was unaware of the object's spatial surroundings, or the artist was aware of the background, but deliberately chose to ignore it.

## Volumetric Spaces

Volumetric space may be detected by the nature of the surfaces revealed within the whole of a rendering. When its background shows only literal, objective surfaces, a rendering portrays objects in volumetric space. The overall space depicted in Figure 7–2 is literal and objective because it is defined by a literal kitchen wall and a literal tabletop. The background of a rendered volumetric space is neither open to the sky nor is it undefined; rather, it is made up of substantial, measurable walls and surfaces.

Architectural paraline drawings describe objects in volumetric space. In every paraline drawing, all measurements are made to scale, and all lines and edges that are parallel to each other in reality are constructed so that they are parallel to each other in the drawing. An example of a paraline drawing of a cube is illustrated in Figure 9–3. Each face of this cube is constructed with edges that parallel one of the cube's three principle axes.

A cube drawn to scale in paraline may be freely shifted up or down, left or right, without having to modify its shape and size. If the cube isn't rotated, it retains its exact shape no matter where it is located in the pictorial space. Another cube of the same size and shape can be added anywhere in the drawing. This cannot be done in perspective drawings.

A cube constructed in paraline has zero vanishing points. Compared to a cube constructed in a perspective with one or more vanishing points, a paraline cube is more self-contained, has a stronger center of gravity, and is less influenced by its surrounding context. In a perspective rendering, the shape and size of a cube changes depending upon where the cube is located

***Figure** 7–2.*   Objective space: *A white cardboard scale model with eight columns rests on a kitchen table. The model is understood in the same literal and three-dimensional terms as the toaster and wall tiles in the background.*

**Figure 7–3.** Objective space: *Literal objects that we can touch with our hands, objects like scale rulers and cardboard models, like potatoes and cheese cutters, may be interpreted in objective space.*

in the pictorial space. The influence of the surrounding perspective field is responsible for these changes.

Intuitively, three-dimensional objects perceived as having parallel, nonconverging lines may be interpreted to be extreme foreground material. Paraline visual fields effectively capture small scale, near objects in volumetric space.

## The Pictorial Interpretation

*So art is limited to the infinite, and beginning there cannot progress.*

JAMES WHISTLER

Pictorial realism emphasizes the overall structure of the rendering's middle ground pictorial space, not the individual objects and features that occupy this space.

In this second spatial zone, we must first of all have an idea about how we want to organize the whole of the rendering's physical space, then we can introduce objects into the scene so that they fit into the space—not the other way around. Because the shape of the pictorial space is decided upon beforehand, the buildings and trees that we introduce into the scene may undergo size and shape changes depending upon where they are located in the pictorial depth of field.

The renderer, in switching from a near objective to a middle pictorial interpretation of the visual field, loses the ability to freely move objects around in the pictorial space. But this loss is more than offset by a gain in ability to express the entire depth and breadth of the pictorial space itself.

In the theater of realism, perspective or atmospheric effects can only be physically represented if the space of the middle stage is compressed or attenuated. This compression, i.e., the enclosure of the stage on three sides, imposes a limitation: the scene can only be viewed by the audience from one side. In exchange for this limitation of viewing direction, the audience gains greater depth and breadth of visual field: everything from table and chair in the foreground to horizon line and sky in the background can be depicted in the scene.

This manner of viewing the middle ground space also imposes restrictions on the way that a stage set may be illuminated. Side lighting is possible. Further, a source of light located in the background will cast accurate shade and shadows. However, it is technically difficult to cast shadows so that they appear to move into the distance rather than toward the viewer.

The middle zone may be envisioned to consist of three overlapping yet distinctly different interpretations of space:

## Perspective Space

The main point of the 15th-century reinvention of linear perspective was not to make pictures look more real to the observer. Rather, it was to introduce a method of drawing that would allow the artist to translate objects from one spatial language into another. In other words, perspective structure, considered as a system, is what makes it possible for the experienced renderer to shuffle objects back and forth between volumetric and pictorial space. With perspective, the plans and elevations of an object modelled in volumetric space can be projected into pictorial space.

Linear perspective causes parallel lines to converge and proportions to diminish in depth of space (Figures 7–4, 7–5). Only through the steady, measured recession of these depth intervals is the viewer of a scene able to grasp the illusion of an infinite spatial depth. But perspective constructions that define buildings and sidewalks with precision and clarity in the foreground and midground of a pictorial space define nothing in the distant background.

The logical conventions of linear perspective are utterly dependent on an exact center, referred to as a station point. The various geometries of linear perspective unfold away from this fixed point, whenever it may be located within the visual field. Remove the point, and the perspective structure collapses.

Philipo Brunelleschi, an Italian architect, is credited with the 15th-century rediscovery of the principles of classical perspective. Leon Battista Alberti wrote the earliest description of its principles. Since that time, artists and mathematicians have written about, refined, and refuted its principles.

In garden art, the ideal mid-16th-century Italian garden included the vista, which was a tree-lined avenue terminating at a point in the extreme distance. Like perspective, the vista can dominate the foreground of a rendering. We may feel surrounded by it. From this foreground staging platform, the vista hurls its parallel walls headlong into the depths of pictorial space, only to be reduced to a vanishing point in the extreme distance by the steady, relentless expansion of the surrounding pictorial space. A splendid 16th-century vista can be found in the Boboli Garden in Florence (Figure 6–3).

## Gravitational Space

*There is a property in the horizon which no man has but he whose eye can integrate all the parts, that is, the poet.*

RALPH WALDO EMERSON

The distant horizon line, an important element in the typical eye-level perspective view, cannot be explained in terms of linear perspective alone. The horizon line is the result of the earth's gravity. Linear perspective does not explain gravity. In the eye-level perspective, it is gravitational space that accounts for the sky above and the earth's ground plane below (Figures 7–6, 7–7).

The experienced renderer understands the subtle ways that this fundamental spatial field can affect the shape of features as they recede into the depth of the pictorial space. In general, the deeper the depicted space, the more pronounced the influence of gravity. Hard-edged highly differentiated shapes in the foreground tend to fuse into soft, undulating horizontal bands in the pictorial distance. In the gravitational space, depth of field filters out verticals. Tree trunks in the foreground dissolve into horizontal treelines in the extreme background. In that regard, the horizon may be interpreted as the deepest visual line in the pictorial view. Orientation of objects is affected by gravitational space. A cube which may appear at various angles in the near becomes upright and anchors to the ground with increasing depth of field.

The purpose of the ideal 17th-century French formal garden was to dominate gravitational space. The ground plane and horizon line were the major natural features of the landscape to be organized in the garden's layout and design. At Vaux le Vicomte, the garden's main prospect terminated not on a point at infinity, but on an artificial horizon line (Figure 6–5).

## Aerial Space

The descriptive powers of linear perspective are no match for the enormous complexity and unfathomable mysteries of living organic physical contexts.

**Figure 7–4.** Perspective pictorial space: *The model of an objective space depicted in Figure 7–2 is extended to include a perspective pictorial middle distance. The columns in the constructed perspective space diminish in size as they recede into the depths of the model's pictorial space toward the kitchen wall just beyond the toaster.*

**Figure 7—5.** Perspective pictorial space: *Once the modelled interpretation of objective space commits itself to a middle pictorial distance, the model itself may be viewed from only one side.*

*Figure* 7–6. Gravitational pictorial space: *The model's pictorial space expands in depth to include an extended horizon line. The wing-like extensions on either side of the model express the inclusion of gravitational pictorial space.*

*Figure* 7–7.   *This rendering portrays objective and pictorial interpretations of space. In the foreground, both the white cardboard columns and the scale-model person are in three-dimensional objective space. Further back into the scene, beyond the model's proscenium arch, forced perspective coexists with gravitational pictorial space. The plant and the dining room chair behind the model, in the background of the rendered scene, both exist in objective space.*

The trees and clouds and other assorted random organic debris of true nature will forever elude complete analytic description. To flesh out the missing contextural pieces of middle ground pictorial space requires yet another even broader and less restrictive interpretation of pictorial depth. Call it aerial space. This third type of pictorial space captures the textural continuity and expansiveness of the middle ground pictorial space.

In this third kind of space, the whole of the depicted scene may be envisioned as a kind of huge outdoor room or cave. In contrast to perspective, aerial pictorial space is organized around the idea of an open, indefinite center which is itself contained within a closed, coherent background shell.

In aerial space, it is the continuity of the background that organizes the diverse features in the foreground, not the other way around. Aerial space is based on the common-sense observation that with increasing depth of pictorial space, the everyday chaotic clutter of the foreground with its lawn mower handles, sticky ice-cream cones, and discarded gum wrappers dissolves in stages toward the unity of a background surface of no visual contrast. Depth filters out contrasts hierarchically.

The depth and breadth of this pictorial space is either traced or rendered intuitively to communicate the generalized feeling of loss of detail. Devices for capturing its effects include gradation of tone and the gradual changing of one shape into another. Atmospheric effects may be expressed in terms of fog or smog. If the space is defined through luminous effects, it will appear flatter.

In the 18th and early 19th centuries, a time when romanticism in the arts flourished, the English mastered this type of space. The landscape paintings of John Constable and Joseph Mallord William Turner reflect a concern for aerial and atmospheric effects. In garden art, Stourhead Garden, layered out in the mid-18th century, is organized around the principles of aerial or attenuated space (Figure 6–7).

## Shared Attributes of the Three Pictorial Spaces

Common to all three types of middle-ground pictorial space is the idea of modelling infinite space in the round. The perspective is built round the station point from the inside out; the aerial space is built from the textural enclosing shell of the background toward a center of indefinite location.

In addition, each spatial interpretation assumes that the surface of the rendering's paper is like a window. The viewer sees deep pictorial space through the illusion of the rendering's transparent picture plane.

# The Optical Interpretation

*It has been pointed out [that] the artist, with his problem of making a unitary picture out of his complicated ideas of the three-dimensional, is compelled to separate clearly the two-dimensional appearance of the object from the general subjective idea of depth. The total volume of a picture will then consist, according to the objects represented, of a greater or lesser number of such imaginary layers arranged one behind the other, yet all together uniting into one appearance having one uniform depth measurement. So the artist divides and groups his ideas of space and form. . . .*

ADOLPH VON HILDEBRAND

Optical realism substitutes parallel frontal planes for the modelling of form and space in the round. It creates a visual world where there are no depth planes.

In the transition from middle to far pictorial space, something is lost: namely, a palpable sense of pictorial depth, but this loss of depth is more than offset by a gain in lateral continuity and expansiveness.

Toward the back of the theater of realism's stage, we find the flat backdrop. Strange as it may seem, the only plausible explanation for the most distant background in the rendering's pictorial view is that it is flat as this backdrop. In theory, the stage's backdrop represents the distant surface "beyond roundness." Immanuel Kant eloquently described the limits of a "rounded" pictorial depth when he stated, ". . . there is no end but an abyss of real immensity in presence of which all the capability of human conception sinks exhausted."

This is indeed a very large pictorial space. However, and this is important, no matter how immensely large we may envision a pictorial space, it will remain limited, bound by its own definition to the depiction of unambiguous progressions into depth. On the other hand, because its depth is by definition ambiguous, the flat background plane is more open to interpretation in depth than pictorial space and therefore has the potential to be deeper.

The unique properties of the flat background can be interpreted in many interesting ways. For example, if the deepest conceivable background plane in a rendered scene is totally flat, then, in the absence of foreground and middle-ground features, what is to distinguish it from the surface of the drawing paper itself? The answer, of course, is that we are often unable to distinguish between near and far in this field. Depth is ambiguous.

For the past century, many artists have not been interested in painting grand illusions of spatial depth. Instead, they have generally preferred to work in a flatness devoid of spatial depth. George Seurat, a late 19th century optical painter, used thousands of small dots or short dashed lines in composing his works. Seurat's works were more explorations of the color interactions of painted points on the surface of the canvas than experiments in extending the boundaries of pictorial depth of field.

Cubist painters expressed spatial depth ambiguously. In *Guernica*, Pablo Picasso made use of transparency to negate the overlap necessary to clarify spatial depth. The clear articulation of one object in front of another gave way to indeterminant relative depth positions of elements within paintings. Juan Gris's *Landscape at Cerett* has little sense of pictorial depth. The painting looks as if it were made by pasting random layers of magazine clippings to the canvas, although even this depth clue is not applied consistently across the surface of the canvas.

The deepest depth plane is, in its extreme interpretation, somewhat akin to what Gestalt psychologists refer to as the state of minimum visual stimulation, an undifferentiated unfocusable fog. The psychologist J.J. Gibson defines a similar kind of background. In his book, *The Perception of the Visual World*, he asserts that there is no such thing as perception of space without a continuous background surface.

In terms of stage set design, there are three types of flat, background spaces.

## Layered Space

The most tangible interpretation of the background is that it is made up of layered space. We see evidence of this in the distant mountains which appear to layer. We see this kind of space when looking out the side window of a moving car. Features in the landscape appear to slide by each other in definite spatial layers.

Overlap is layered space's key depth indicator. Overlap lets us know

**Figure 7–8.** Aerial perspective and layered space: *The model's distant cardboard treeline silhouettes against the kitchen wall's green plastic tiles. The model's flat cardboard cutout trees are examples of layered optical spatial interpretations. Light and atmospheric effects lend this rendering a generalized focus and sense of depth and surround. The model's distant background sky is undefined.*

***Figure* 7–9.**    *The proscenium arch from the model in Figure 7–7 is removed. A photograph of a continuous background is placed behind the model. The model's depth of field is now complete. Movement into the rendering's depth of field proceeds from the near, objective foreground world of potatoes, columns and scale rulers into a middle-distance world of perspective, gravitational and aerial spatial interpretations. The scene terminates in the distance with layered and screened optical interpretations of space.*

which plane is in front of the other, but it does not tell us how much distance separates each plane.

In the theater of realism, toward the back of the stage, just before the backdrop, the stage may consist of layers of cutout backdrops (Figure 7–8).

In stage set design, each depth plane in layered space can be illuminated separately, but there may be no shade and shadow within the layered planes themselves.

## Masked Space

In the theater of realism, masked space is found in luminous mat paintings. In this space, if we can call it that, the depicted scene is literally embedded in the plane of the backdrop. The thing that makes this "space" unique is that some painted areas of the backdrop are translucent while other areas are opaque. Because of this, the mat painting can be illuminated in a variety of different ways. For example, if a luminous mat painting is back lit, the transparent portion of the painting will glow in comparison to the opaque part. It goes without saying that considerable realism can be achieved in this space alone. Much of the spatial effect of a luminous mat painting is dependent on large-scale night/day lighting effects. Silhouette and mood can be varied in this spatial zone.

In 1822, Louis Daguerre invented the Diorama, which was a kind of early version of today's movie theater. As stated in Daguerre's English patent application, the Diorama represented "an improved Mode of publicly exhibiting Pictures or Painted Scenery of every Description and of distributing or directing the Day Light upon through them, so as to produce many beautiful or Effects of Light and Shade." Daguerre's painted scenery consisted of large-scale luminous mat paintings. These paintings literally came to life under various transmitted and reflected lighting conditions. They captured with surprising realism the momentary changes of mood characteristic of outdoor space. Fittingly, Daguerre invented the Daguerreotype, a kind of photograph, not long thereafter.

## Screened Space

Screened space, or flat space, is grasped in both three and two dimensions simultaneously. In actual experience, screened space is the backyard as it appears through the mesh of a screen door. The door's metal screen is two-dimensional. The backyard is three-dimensional. The surface of the screen door's fine metal mesh veils the space of the backyard. Depending on how we focus our eyes on the scene, we may see more of the screen and less of the backyard, or more of the backyard and less of the flat metal screen.

Screened space may be modelled in three dimensions and two dimensions simultaneously. In Figure 7–1, screened space is represented by the photograph of dark trees and sky behind the Roman arch, in the background of the modelled scene. Because the illusion of space is contained in the plane of a photograph and not modelled in three dimensions, this screened space is two-dimensional. On the other hand, because we see spatial depth in the photograph, the same screened space is three-dimensional. It is worth noting here that we could model the imagery in this background photograph in three dimensions, but we choose instead to interpret the scenery in the flat plane of a photograph.

Screened space may also be rendered in three and two dimensions simultaneously. The renderer pushes the spatial imagery within a drawing toward a flat screen by emphasizing breadth of drawing surface over illusion of spatial depth. This may be accomplished in a number of different ways. The background in Figure 7–9, for example, was rendered as screened space. The spatial illusion of clouds in the sky was illustrated with screenlike 45° line strokes. The consistent application of 45° line strokes veiled the three-dimensional illusion of clouds and pushed the sky into a broader, duller, flatter, more distant, and vague visual impression.

## The Total Visual Field

*Nature hastens to render account of herself to the mind. Classification begins.*
RALPH WALDO EMERSON

The theater of realism's stage may consist of as many as three types of spatial interpretations: objective, pictorial, and optical. Regardless of how many different kinds of spatial interpretations there are on the stage, or, for that matter, how they are organized, one thing must remain constant: from the vantage point of an audience member viewing the stage, the scene must appear to fuse together into a single coherent image. The pencil rendering works in much the same way. It may be interpreted as the unified image of three distinct spatial interpretations. The finished rendering is the fusion of these three different interpretations of space.

## Spaces Within Spaces

The seamless continuity of a finished rendering may hide the fact that it was actually drawn with three separate spatial interpretations in mind (Figures 7–10, 7–11). When the subject matter of a rendering is divided into separate spatial zones for the purpose of organizing the rendering depth of field, the zones themselves become subsets of one overall image.

Assuming the rendering is interpreted in this way, as spaces within spaces, then how are these spaces organized? The objective, pictorial, and optical may be arranged in strict order, one following the other into the extreme depth of the pictorial space. The renderer's decision as to where to draw the line that separates each spatial zone is open to interpretation. On the other hand, the coherence of a rendered image is not affected if the three spatial interpretations are not in strict order or clearly demarcated. On the stage, for example, the three spatial zones may overlap. Layered space may exist in objective space. Layered space often appears in the extreme foreground of renderings. In the theatrical stage set, the proscenium arch itself is an example of a foreground layered plane. Layered landscape imagery and pictorial architectural imagery may both occupy the middle ground. The tree tends toward symmetry. The tree looks essentially the same from all sides. On the other hand, the building tends to look different depending upon how it is oriented. Symmetrical forms tend to collapse into layered space before asymmetrical shapes.

The continuity of the total rendered image is not affected if the space of the physical stage collapses into two or fewer spatial zones. The stage may consist of the objective and the optical with no intervening pictorial interpretation. This does not affect the appearance of the final image. What changes is the renderer's grasp of the spatial implications of the depicted scene, which is reflected in an ability to physically model it.

## Conclusion

Though renderers have always subscribed to the theory that the rendered image expresses the modelled one, it is nonetheless possible to render scenes in which appearance and reality do not square. Whenever the rendered image conceals rather than expresses directly the "mind's construction" we have irony. It seems with realism as our goal, irony prevents us from ever truly describing the totality of the actual viewing experience. Imagination has so far always dissolved our categories.

**Figure 7–10.** The total visual field: Overview of model depicted in Figure 7–11. *This model includes a near objective foreground, a middle-distance perspective pictorial space, and far optical interpretations of space.*

***Figure 7–11.*** The total visual field: Spectator's eye-view into the modelled world depicted in Figure 7–10. *Objective, optical, and pictorial interpretations of space appear to fuse together. Here, literal features in objective space such as the wall in the right foreground coordinate visually with elements modelled in pictorial and optical space. Note the two interpretations of perspective: One interpretation of perspective is physically modelled in pictorial space. The other, contained in the photograph of the archway, is in the model's optical space.*

# Chapter 8

# The Gentle Art of Persuading the Viewer

*There is nothing ugly; I never saw an ugly thing in my life: for let the form of an object be what it may,—light, shade and perspective will always make it beautiful.*

JOHN CONSTABLE

*The artist should once and forever emancipate himself from the bondage of appearance and the unpardonable sin of expending on ignoble aims the precious ointment that should serve only to nourish the lamp burning before the tabernacle of his muse.*

ALBERT PINKHAM RYDER

*A picture is something which requires as much knavery, trickery and deceit as the perpetration of a crime. Paint falsely and then add the accent of nature.*

EDGAR DEGAS

The sidewalk trembles with the passing of a mass transit bus. A greasy cloud of diesel exhaust trails behind, stinging pedestrian eyes. The smell of sun-baked creosote drifts from a telephone pole; its pungent odor adulterates the gentle, inviting smells wandering from a bakery doorway. On the sidewalk a piece of discarded gum, soft from the warm day, interrupts the click-clack of high heeled shoes; a woman curses, spearmint-flavored strands trailing from her heel. Reminders of nature, a tree here, a grassy lot there, add color to the concrete, brick and billboard-infested urban street scene.

This written description of the street scene depicted in Figure 8–13 captures the sights, sounds and smells of a particular moment on the day the picture was taken. In rendering, as in writing, the art of persuading the viewer begins with the illustrator's ability to coax specific relevant facts and details out of even the most ordinary of settings.

Beyond the facts, however, even the most realistic-looking rendering is riddled with the renderer's own opinions and values. The most deliberately honest rendering is full of behind-the-scenes decisions that defy easy explanation. In every perspective rendering, judgements are made regarding the observer's angle and direction of view, choice of foreground features, quality of illumination, type of composition, and desired overall mood. It is with these fuzzy attributes of the rendering that this chapter is primarily devoted.

The gentle art of persuading the viewer embraces both the familiar and the conventional. On the other hand, it warns against relying on style and convention alone. Rendering styles and conventions are useful. At the same time, it never hurts to twist things around once in a while. By convention we render the view of a building in broad daylight without bothering to consider depicting the scene at twilight or as if the building is on fire under the light of the moon.

Rendered realism of the kind depicted in this book is sometimes assumed to reflect only literal thinking. Nothing could be further from the truth. In fact, every pencil rendering in this book can be abstracted into more than one layer. Each layer of abstraction can be expressed in terms of a visual diagram. Each diagram isolates one specific attribute of the rendering.

Behind the scenes, the task of putting together persuasive renderings is dry and technical. Diagrams are the dry and technical visual means by which the renderer analyzes a drawing's underlying structure and organization. This chapter describes the kinds of diagrams that went into making the renderings for this book.

# Diagramming

As we struggle by fits and starts to render a building or landscape, our minds switch to different modes of interpretation. In one mode, our eyes filter out everything in the drawing and we see only the texture of the pencil stroke on paper. In another mode, we see only the abstract pattern of lights and darks on the surface of the paper. In yet another mode, we are in tune only with the sense of spatial depth in the composition. Sometimes, our mind's eye focuses on specific detail and literalness of interpretation. In each mode, we isolate one aspect of the drawing for the purpose of asking ourselves questions about it: How does it feel? Is it balanced? Does it feel balanced to itself and to other modes?

Rendered realism is only partly the result of craftsman-like dexterity. Other factors contribute to the sense of realism in a drawing. These factors, analogous to the modes of thought described above, can be diagrammed. Here are eight useful variations.

## Massing Diagrams

Crisply contoured masses like soup cans and coffee cups have greater visual presence in renderings than flat, planar shapes. Solid, rounded forms appear to advance; flat shapes appear to recede. Massing diagrams emphasize the rendering's three-dimensional figural solids. The pattern of voids that surround these solids are as important to evaluate as the solids themselves (Figures 8–1, 8–2).

## Pictorial Space Diagrams

William Turner's paintings were once described by Constable as "airy visions painted with steam." Turner's paintings were, in effect, pure pictorial space diagrams. A pictorial space diagram describes the overall shape of a rendering's pictorial depth of field (Figures 8–3, 8–4). We may diagram the pictorial space of a rendering by "melting" all of the hard edges of its subject matter into a continuum of pure curving surfaces. The diagram is not complete until everything in the scene looks as if it is cut from the same bolt of cloth, or, softer yet, until the objects have dematerialized, blurred into a state of cloud-like, hazy, misty, vaporous "steam."

Like a cave, with its stalagmites and stalactites, pictorial space diagrams capture a primitive sense of spatial enclosure; a sort of pure state of insideness. This generalized feeling of insideness is not limited to the spatial diagramming of indoor rooms. Pictorial space diagrams can be used to model outdoor landscape scenes as well. It is possible, for instance, using pictorial space diagrams, to gently contour clouds and landscape features in such a way that the whole outdoor space takes on the subtle shape of the inside of a cave.

To see the forms in the cave, we must illuminate them. Sources of illumination are chosen so as to bring out the desired generalized character of the overall space. Indoors, where illumination is provided by artificial lighting, placement and intensity of light sources affects the look of the scene. Out of doors, the renderer's decision as to where to position the sun in the sky affects the overall appearance of the space.

## Tonal Contrast Diagrams

If pictorial space diagrams are soft and flowing, tonal contrast diagrams are just the opposite: hard and stone-like. Tonal contrast diagrams flatten the subject matter of renderings into crisp fragments of lights against darks.

*Figure 8–1.* *Massing diagram. The rounded solid forms in Figure 8–1 are shown against a neutral background. Pencil strokes emphasize the solid contours of the masses. Shapes of the residual spaces, the white voids, are balanced against these solids.*

*Figure 8–2.* *Cups, cans, and vegetables, things we can grip in our hand, are examples of solid, figural masses.*

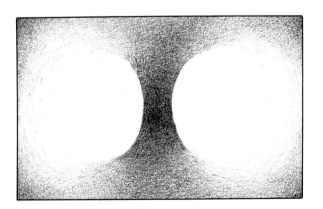

*Figure 8–3.* *Pictorial space diagram. The leaves, bark, and roots of the tree in Figure 8–4 are subtly modelled so that they fit within the overall cave-like shape of the space expressed above.*

*Figure 8–4.* *Gnarled tree in garden at Dumbarton Oaks, Washington, D.C.*

There are three basic kinds of tonal diagrams: (1) figure/ground; (2) high-contrast; and (3) stepped tonal contrast.

The distinction between the first two diagrams is subtle, but significant. Figure/ground and high-contrast diagrams are both made up of pure lights against darks. What varies is their interpretation. Figure/ground diagrams are assumed to have depth. In them, figures are subjectively perceived to stand out against a background, which is assumed to pass underneath or behind. The high-contrast diagram, on the other hand, is meant to be grasped as a flat-pattern arrangement of lights and darks. The third type of diagram, the stepped tonal contrast diagram, consists of not two but three or more flat shades of gray. For example, black, middle gray, and white.

## Figure/Ground Diagrams

Around 1910, psychologists Max Wertheimer, Wolfgang Kohler, and Kurt Koffka made the distinction between figure and ground an important criterion in Gestalt (form) theory. In their view, a clearly recognizable visual whole, or gestalt, could only be perceived if it stood out as a figure against background. In connection with the diagramming of renderings, it is to be noted that the impression of an entire landscape scene can be created out of nothing but the figure/ground arrangement of black and white shapes on the surface of a piece of paper (Figures 8–5, 8–6). It stands to reason, therefore, that if we can see the subject mater of a rendering in its figure/ground diagram, we can identify which of the visual features are most likely to be spontaneously grouped by the mind in order to form generalized entities, or gestalts. Some forms, or gestalts, are bound to be stronger than others. We can change the strength of these gestalts in order to achieve a desired compositional balance.

Figure/ground diagrams are not new. The term "blot drawing," for example, was coined by Alexander Cozens, an 18th-century English watercolorist, to describe a technique to spontaneously create pleasing landscape scenes. To create a blotscape, he recommended crumpling a sheet of paper, smoothing it, then, while thinking of landscapes, blot the paper with ink, using as little conscious control as possible. Cozens discovered, as da Vinci had before him, that the particulars of a landscape scene may follow from accidental ink smears on the page. The idea behind Cozens' technique was to create chance effects on purpose, to fuse accident with design. Random blots suggested images. The artist could search for real scenes that resembled the blot pattern, substituting actual vegetation for the pattern of black

tone. Or, the artist could simply translate the tonal blot pattern into landscape imagery from memory alone. Key to the success of Cozens' technique was the fact that the mind's eye is able to form gestalts, to see well-formed landscapes in seemingly random figure/ground patterns.

## High-Contrast Diagrams

High-contrast diagrams are meant to be interpreted as pure flat-pattern design. They satisfy nothing more than a basic, primitive urge on our part to visually balance the arrangement of lights and darks on the rendering's surface (Figures 8–7, 8–8). Because these diagrams are so superficial, people are often tempted to search for deeper meaning in them, to see them in figure/ground. But it is the total shallowness of the high-contrast diagram that makes it such a valuable diagramming tool. The diagram isn't supposed to communicate anything other than itself, so in that sense it is unbiased toward subject matter. Developing an eye for it allows us to undercut every conceivable arrangement of figures imaginable. Organic forms like trees, clouds, and other complex shapes, can be easily balanced in the rendering. Everything from homemade snapshots of grandma and the kids to nonobjective paintings can be scrutinized with high-contrast diagrams.

To envision this field even as we look at realistic renderings, as a matter of course, every drawing should undergo an eye-squint test. This test consists in squinting the eyes until the details of what we see are reduced to a pattern of blur. If the blurry impression feels unbalanced or uninteresting, no amount of refinement will save the drawing.

In the 19th century, John Ruskin observed: "Of course the character of everything is best manifested by Contrast . . . light is exhibited by darkness, darkness by light." Sixty years later, Arthur Guptill wrote: "Now a pen drawing, when thought of in the simplest way, is nothing but a [complex] spot on a sheet of paper." Guptill asked: "Is the pattern or arrangement of spots for the entire rendering interesting? Is it pleasing?" In other words, do the smaller spots contribute to the overall effect? He concludes that there is an endless variety of spotting arrangements for all masses remaining fixed in position.

The recognition that spots may be pleasing in their own right is evidenced in the writings of famous painters. Alfred Sisley, the impressionist painter, observed: "Every picture shows a spot in which the artist himself has fallen in love."

*Figure 8–5.* *Figure/ground diagram.*

*Figure 8–6.* *Skipper Bud's pier, Milwaukee, Wisconsin.*

*Figure 8–7.* *High-contrast diagram.*

*Figure 8–8.* *Rhododendrons, Broad Walk, the Royal Botanic Gardens, Kew Palace, London.*

**Stepped Tonal Contrast Diagrams**    A high-contrast diagram broken into flat tonal values consisting of three or more shades of gray becomes a stepped tonal contrast diagram (Figures 8–9, 8–10). The more tonal steps, the greater the acuity of the diagram.

Here is a rule of thumb that applies to all forms of tonal diagrams: If all of a finished rendering's tonal values, ranging from black to white, could be scraped from the page and mixed together like paint, a balanced tonal effect is achieved if the resulting mixture averages to 50 percent gray. For example, if half of the surface area of a finished rendering is black, the other half white, the average is 50 percent, which is balanced. The same holds true if the surface area is divided into equal portions of black, middle gray, and white. If all of the tonal values add up to more than 50 percent gray, say, 75 percent, the rendering is said to be in a low key. Low-key renderings are dark. A rendering is high key when the overall tone is light, less than 50 percent.

## Composition Diagrams

How we choose to frame or crop the subject matter of a composition is open to interpretation. Do we compose the rendering so that it includes the total view of a building or just a portion of it? Do we depict the scene in wide or narrow field of vision? Do we compose the scene for artless or stylistic effect? William Gilpin, in his *Three Essays on Picturesque Beauty*, written in 1794, had this to say about composing buildings in the landscape: "A piece of Palladian architecture may be elegant in the last degree, but if we introduce it in a picture it immediately becomes a formal object and ceases to please. Should we wish to give it picturesque beauty . . . we must beat down one half of it, deface the other, and throw the mutilated members round in heaps. In short from a smooth building we must turn it

into a rough ruin. No painter who had the choice of the two objects would hesitate which to chuse."

Needless to say, Gilpin's compositional advice is firmly rooted in his own strong point of view. Without benefit of this point of view, his picturesque thoughts on composition would have lacked focus. Advanced compositional theory requires point of view. Obviously, a detailed discussion of various compositional points of view is well beyond the scope of this book. About all that can be said here is that it is a good idea to study the wide-ranging theories and works of other artists and delineators in the field.

Generally speaking, compositions are either formal or informal. Formal compositions balance symmetrically. An overall composition may be formally symmetrical, but this does not preclude the possibility of local asymmetries. In other words, a formal composition does not have to be totally formal down to the last blade of grass. To achieve informal balance, photographers and delineators often compose their pictures according to the rule of thirds (Figures 8–11, 8–12). The frame is divided into nine parts. The picture's center of visual interest is located near the intersection of horizontal and vertical lines at 1/3 points of the picture. Another method of dividing a frame for the purpose of achieving an informal balance is based on the golden section or golden mean.

The golden mean is expressed in the ratio 1: 1.6180339, or 1:.6180339. The ratios are equivalent. A rectangle whose long side is 1.618 times the length of the short side is called a golden mean rectangle. The golden mean rectangle when combined in various ways with the square generates dynamically balanced compositional grids.

Lines or contours that carry through the composition are called strong lines. The ocean's horizon line, if it crosses the entire frame, a tree trunk in the foreground that originates below the frame and extends above it, are both examples of strong lines. The harmonies and tensions that develop between horizontal, diagonal, and vertical lines can be diagrammed.

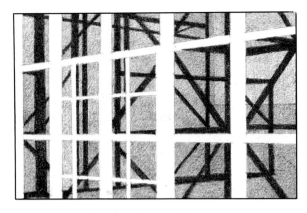

Figure 8–9.   Stepped tonal contrast diagram.

Figure 8–10.   The building in the background is hidden behind the framework of another building under construction.

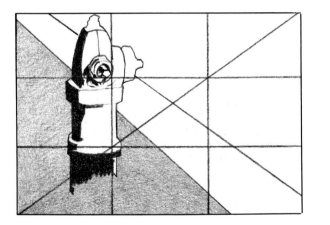

Figure 8–11.   Composition diagram.

Figure 8–12.   Fire hydrant framed according to the rule of thirds.

## Symbolic Imagery Diagrams

Symbolic imagery can be diagrammed (Figure 8–13). Some visual imagery is attractive or repulsive to look at while other imagery is dull or weak. Excessively strong or novel imagery often meets with as much rejection as imagery which is unrelentingly repeated. In an optimal rendering, emphasis will fall slightly toward the new in order to elicit attention and interest. Bear in mind the obvious fact that something new to one person may be familiar and redundant to another.

On a subtler level, the rendering's subject matter can be described in terms of character, place, and mood. The untrained eye is often attracted to or swayed by the literal attributes of the rendering—its obvious, overt imagery. Often overlooked by the untrained eye is the impact that sense of place and mood may have in shaping the rendering's overall emotional effect.

## Casting Features in Their Best Light

There is no single best way to illuminate the subject matter of rendering. The renderer in fact always has a certain degree of latitude in establishing the mood and tonal balance of a rendering even before committing to the refinement of detail. Here is where tonal contrast diagrams are useful. By using these diagrams during the early planning stages of a drawing, the renderer can save considerable time and frustration later on. Depth of field, balance, and mood can be worked out beforehand in these preliminary tonal sketches.

## Tonal Patterns Coordinated With the Illumination of Pictorial Space

The eye of the viewer is attracted to areas of crisp, fragmented shapes in high tonal contrast. On the other hand, the viewer's eye tends to glaze over when it is forced to stare for long periods of time at areas of gray in low tonal contrast and indistinct outline. It stands to reason that if a visually compelling tonal contrast arrangement can be coordinated with a realistic illumination of subject matter, then we will have integrated visual interest with a realistic interpretation of pictorial space.

High tonal contrast, which attracts the eye, can be symbolized as W/B, white against black. Low tonal contrast, dull and boring to the eye, can be symbolized as G, gray. With this basic distinction in mind, it is possible to coordinate the overall pattern of lights and darks with the illumination of an overall pictorial space. Here are four basic types of tonal contrast patterns: W/B, white against black; W-B, from white to black; W/B-G, from white against black to middle gray; and G-W/B-G, gray to white against black to gray. Pictorial illumination conditions that match up with each contrast pattern are described below.

**Figure** 8–13.    *Symbolic imagery diagram: Street signs prevail on Oakland Avenue, Milwaukee.*

## White Against Black: W/B

The finished rendering may take on the stark appearance of a high-contrast or figure/ground diagram (Figure 8–14). To achieve this crisp yet rather severe effect, we may assume that hard directional light molds the shape of depicted features through strong shade and shadow.

## White Foreground to Black Background: W-B

This tonal-contrast pattern describes a pictorial space that is illuminated by a source of light coincident with the point from which it is viewed (Figure 8–15). In this space, it is assumed that, like light radiating from a bulb, the intensity of the source of illumination diminishes as the square of its distance from the viewer's eye. In the perfect case, where the source of light coincides exactly with the viewer's vantage point, there could be no visible shade or shadow. If every feature in the depicted scene has the same intrinsic surface value, a precise, measurable spatial depth can be constructed.

In the rendering, the distance from the viewer to every point on a surface directly relates to the point's gray value. The darker the gray of the surface point, the greater the distance from the point to the viewer. A gray scale can be made to calibrate depth in terms of degree of gray. This kind of lighting emphasizes overall spatial form. Local distinctions in form and shape are negligible. The viewer is locked into the middle of the scene, at position pure white. Driving at night by the headlights of a car approximates this tonal illumination effect.

## White Against Black Foreground to Gray Background: W/B-G

This tonal-contrast pattern may be interpreted in pictorial depth to consist of sharp high-tonal contrast in the foreground gradually diminishing to no contrast in the background (Figure 8–16). Aerial and atmospheric illumination create this effect. In this type of rendered pictorial space, depth is assumed to filter out tonal contrast. All tonal conditions are possible in the foreground, but the singular condition of no tonal contrast, embodied in the flat, gray coherent surface of deepest depth, is the limiting feature in the background. In photography, backlighting the subject matter approximates this tonal pattern.

## Gray Foreground to White/Black Midground to Gray Background: G-W/B-G

This tonal contrast pattern works well with spot illumination of subject matter (Figure 8–17). The spot tonal effect forces the focus of the drawing toward the midground, where the highest tonal contrast is desired. In many respects, the spot illumination of features in the midground plays into the expectations of the viewer. The building in the midground of the pictorial space is brought into focus through sharp tonal contrast.

In the real world of visual experience, tonal illumination fields combine in various complicated ways. Because of this, the texture of our everyday visual experience is in fact much richer than the four categories listed above.

*Figure 8–14.* *Figure/ground rendering.*

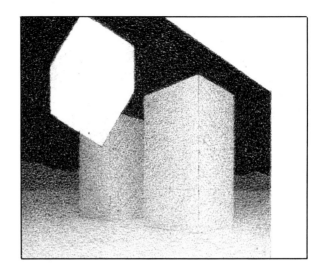

*Figure 8–15.* *Rendered with white foreground to black background.*

*Figure 8–16.* *Rendered with high-contrast foreground to neutral gray background.*

*Figure 8–17.* *Rendered with high-contrast focal emphasis surrounded by lesser tonal contrasts.*

## Focus

The viewer's eye delights in strong tonal contrasts, dark against light. In rendering, then, visual emphasis is achieved by opposing areas of light and dark at the focal point.

Forced focus heightens the emphasis in the rendering of a brick staircase in the Queen's Garden, Kew Palace, London (Figure 8–18). In this rendering, the focus of the drawing is located on the sunlit treads of the brick staircase. It is here that the highest tonal contrast is concentrated. Slightly less intense in tonal contrast but equally as sharp in terms of refinement of detail is the pattern of white mortar joints that make up the brick balustrade. The mortar joint for every baluster, including the upper and lower rail and the pedestal of the staircase, is white.

Surrounding the staircase are areas of lesser detail, finer textural grain, and tonal contrast. The trees in the background are depicted in an almost flat tone, which dilutes their visual contrast with the staircase. The tonal schema for this rendering is shown in the accompanying diagram (Figure 8–19).

## Breadth

The eye glides easily across areas of changing texture but similar tone. John Ruskin described this rendering device as "breadth"—"a large gathering of each kind of thing into one place; light being gathered to light, darkness to darkness, colour to colour."

Figure 8–20 depicts a wall in the Royal Botanical Gardens, Kew Palace, London. Leaning against the brick wall is a white stone fragment resembling a frieze from a classical entablature.

Note how the varied texture of the wall, which is made up of several materials, of brick, rusticated stone, and ivy, nonetheless holds together as a coherent surface, as a visual unity. The various textures of this wall do not fly visually apart into a jumbled visual chaos. It is the constancy of the tone and the consistent coarseness of texture that is diagrammed in Figure 8–21. The wall, with its gray tonal value, serves as a foil for the white stone frieze fragment. The white stone fragment is the visual focus in the center of the composition. Nothing else is this completely white. With regard to this use of white areas, it is advisable to heed Ruskin's comment: a good drawing has ". . . pure white only at the extreme brightest highlights—all else must have tone."

*Figure 8–18.* *Staircase with brick balustrades in the Queen's Garden, Royal Botanic Gardens, Kew Palace, London.*

*Figure 8–19.* *Focus diagram.*

*Figure 8–20.* *The fragment of a classical entablature leans against a wall near Sir William Chamber's Ruined Arch, Royal Botanic Gardens, Kew Palace, London.*

*Figure 8–21.* *Texture diagram.*

## Illumination Effects

The cottage illustrated in Figures 8–22 through 8–25 is situated in Marie Antoinette's Hamlet in the Queen's Garden, Versailles. The same view of the cottage is depicted twice, each under different lighting conditions. Figure 8–22 emphasizes the entry to the cottage through the use of spot illumination. Contrasts of tone and detail are the strongest at the cottage's front door. Because the highest level of contrast and detail is concentrated at the cottage's entry, its two backlit French doors are secondary compositional elements. In Figure 8–24, the front entrance is not spot illuminated, which reduces its level of tonal contrasts. The focal emphasis therefore shifts to the backlit windows because these are now the features with the strongest tonal contrast in the rendering. In both renderings focal emphasis is established through believable illumination effects.

## Silhouette

Silhouetting organizes subject matter into separate spatial depth planes. Under typical daylighting conditions, the sky itself is so bright that features in the landscape often appear somewhat darker in value. Landscape features in the middle distance appear in strong silhouette when the sun is low in the sky. It doesn't matter whether the sun is backlighting the scene or not.

Because the range of values in nature is many times that which can be achieved with black pencil on white paper, renderers must suggest within the limited range of values at their disposal appropriate value contrasts for the natural scenes rendered. In the real world, the sky is bright in comparison to trees. The white of the paper is no match for the actual brightness of a sky, so the trees are made dark to compensate. Silhouettes also emerge in atmospheric perspective. Features such as mountains in the far reaches of pictorial space tend to fade into subtly layered tonal planes silhouetted against each other and the sky.

The background trees in Figure 8–24 are more strongly silhouetted against the sky than the same background trees in Figure 8–22. As a rule-of-thumb, the stronger the silhouette, the brighter and more emphatic the sky appears and the less noticeable the distinction between individual landscape features within the silhouette.

## Grouping of Landscape Features

Features that occur in roughly the same pictorial depth of field can be unified by forcing the constancy of their tones. In Figure 8–23, the foreground, midground, and background features of the rendering group into three distinct tonal layers. This was done to clarify the drawing's overall sense of pictorial space. By comparison, in Figure 8–25, the tonal values of the foreground, midground, and background are nearly constant, thus compressing the sense of depth of its pictorial space.

## Tonal Contrast

The right corner of the cottage in Figure 8–23 is dark against the lighter backdrop of trees. The intensity of the tonal contrast reinforces the spatial separation. In figure 8–25, the tonal contrast between the cottage's right corner and the background trees is equal in intensity but the tonal values of the surfaces are reversed.

*Figure 8–22.*  *Rendering of cottage located in Marie Antoinette's Hamlet, the Queen's Garden, Versailles, France, which emphasizes the entry through use of spot illumination.*

*Figure 8–23.*  *Tonal illumination diagram.*

*Figure 8–24.*  *Rendering of the same cottage in Marie Antoinette's Hamlet, which emphasizes backlit windows.*

*Figure 8–25.*  *Tonal illumination diagram.*

## Forced v. Intrinsic Focus

A forced focus is something added to the basic content of the depicted scene by the delineator as a means of achieving a desired visual effect. An intrinsic focus is built directly into the subject matter of the rendering (Figures 8–26 through 8–29).

The subject matter of a rendering with an intrinsic focus creates its own center of interest. On the other hand, forced focus has nothing to do with subject matter. It is a compositional device that is freely located anywhere in the rendering. Forced focus gives the renderer the power to make absolutely any rendering, no matter how intrinsically ugly, look beautiful. Ultimately, it is the renderer's responsibility to decide whether or not to coordinate forced focus effects with believable sources of illumination.

The view that we see when we look down an avenue toward a terminus has built into it an objective focus. That is, the rendering's pictorial space itself is intrinsically organized around a center of interest. Figure 8–26 provides an example of a rendering with a strong intrinsic focus. The tree-lined alley terminates on the west front of the Petit Trianon. This building dominates the composition by virtue of its commanding position at the end of the alley.

On the other hand, the subject matter of a drawing may be loosely or chaotically organized around nothing in particular, yet the drawing itself may have a strong focus. This is the case in Figure 8–28. The original photograph was a jumble of disconnected forms: house, telephone pole, street, and car. Focus was introduced into the rendering of the photograph by concentrating tonal contrasts and detail toward the center of the composition, on the front porch of the bungalow house.

The diagram of the French vista illustrates a coordinated relationship between objective and subjective foci (Figure 8–27). The focal emphasis of the actual space and the focal emphasis of the drawing's tonal composition are located in the same place in the drawing. On the other hand, the street scene has a subjective but not an objective focus (Figure 8–29).

Forced focus is a powerful rhetorical device. Avoid exaggerating its effect. The rendering will feel too theatrical.

## Continuous Depth of Field

Nicolas Poussin wrote: "A painting will be elegant when the extreme distances are connected to the foregrounds by means of the middle distances in such a way that they will contrast neither too feebly nor with too much harshness of lines and colors." The tonal progression that defines the ground plane in Figure 8–26 blends foreground into background. Often, because of overlap, receding depth planes are hidden from view (Figure 8–22). This results in shallow, compressed, layered pictorial spaces.

## Visual v. Physical Movement Into Depth

Movement into pictorial depth toward a distant goal proceeds along two paths: visual and physical. The visual path toward a destination is straight and direct, as the arrow or crow flies. The physical path, on the other hand, proceeds by the winding, twisted, tortured, thematic movement of the foot as it searches for a way to navigate over physical terrain toward the destination or goal of the depicted scene. The physical path toward a goal takes many different forms. In Figure 8–26, the eye sees the building straight ahead in the extreme distance, yet the foot must veer left or right of the strip of grass in order to reach the building. In Figure 8–28, the front porch of the house, which is the straight-ahead visual goal of the drawing, cannot be reached on foot without traveling around the car in the street.

William Shenstone defines this double movement in his famous maxim: "The foot should never travel by the same path which the eye has traveled over before."

*Figure 8–26.* West front, the Petit Trianon, Versailles.

*Figure 8–27.* Layered tonal contrast diagram.

*Figure 8–28.* House on Vilas Avenue, Madison, Wisconsin.

*Figure 8–29.* Tonal focus diagram.

# Concealment, Contrast and Surprise

William Kent, the 18th-century English landscape designer, once wrote: "All the rules of gardening are reducible to three heads: the contrasts, the management of surprises and the concealment of the bounds." These rules also apply to renderings.

## Concealment of Bounds

Seeking sunlight, the leaves and branches of vegetation in the wilderness of northern Wisconsin tend to grow around and through themselves into tangled thickets of pure visual texture. No abrupt boundaries, stone walls, or cyclone fences interrupt the textural continuity of these landscapes. In places such as residential backyards where artificial boundaries are inevitable but not desired, man-made walls and barriers may be made to blend into the natural landscape if covered with climbing vines or shrubs. In Figure 8–30, the boundary between cottage and ground is concealed. Vines growing on the brick wall of the cottage hide the boundary between cottage and green lawn. The cottage fuses visually with the ground plane because both the vines and the lawn are related tonally. The cottage's vine-covered wall sprouts from the earth like a stalagmite from the floor of a cave. In Figure 8–31, the relation between cottage and ground plane is illustrated with white.

Shelter belts and screens also effectively soften and obscure boundaries. The cottage stands out against a background of trees. These trees form a curtained backdrop, concealing whatever exists behind them. The smooth-ness and tonal uniformity of this background makes it appear as if cut from a single bolt of dark gray cloth.

A backdrop of trees and shrubs defines the winding vista on the grounds of the Boboli Garden in Florence (Figure 8–32). Articulated foreground trees on the left recede into the depths of the pictorial space.

## The Contrasts

The tonal value of the background trees is slightly darker in value where they appear to go behind the edge of the cottage (Figure 8–31). This provides stronger contrast at the drawing's focal emphasis, which is the sharp light/dark contrast along the left corner of the cottage.

## Management of Surprises

The pictorial space in Figure 8–30 is shaped like the swirling vortex of a hurricane. The space in Figure 8–32 is shaped more like a winding open-air tunnel. Yet, despite differences in overall spatial configuration, the focus of both renderings is on a silhouetted edge, an edge that hints at the idea that something lies around the corner.

The source of illumination in Figure 8–33 is obscured by a hill, as if the place where the viewer stands is dark, but there is light beyond the bend. The eye of the spectators seeks tonal contrast and is attracted toward light. The feet will want to go where the eye is attracted. What mystery lies around the silhouetted corner?

*Figure 8–30.* Cottage in Marie Antoinette's Hamlet, the Queen's Garden, Versailles, France.

*Figure 8–31.* Diagram depicting tonal organization of pictorial space.

*Figure 8–32.* Diagram depicting tonal movement into pictorial depth.

*Figure 8–33.* Path behind Cafe-Haus, Boboli Garden, Florence, Italy.

# Chapter 9

# Rendered Realism

*You might object: "Perspective is deceitful, because it shows you something that does not exist." True; nonetheless in a drawing it is truthful because a drawing is not a true thing, either. . . .*

FILARETE

*I desire my conceptions to be preserved in their virginity in my brain.*

GIOVANNI SEGANTINI

*Only when he no longer knows what he is doing does the painter do good things.*

EDGAR DEGAS

The discussion from previous chapters focused primarily on the problem of rendering existing scenery. The question yet remains: how do we apply what we've learned to the rendering of places that do not yet exist? This, of course, is a most important consideration, addressing the very reason we would want to render at all.

Rendering may be defined as the art of showing people how their dreams and wishes will look, depicted in their best light.

In the literary sense, the rendered scene may be envisioned in either of two contexts: fictional or non-fictional. Here, we will assume that people's dreams, in order to be believable, must dwell in familiar settings. In other words, the settings must look real. They must appear to exist in Detroit or Milwaukee, not the Elysian Fields or Utopia.

It stands to reason that in order to create the look of these futuristic realities, the renderer must be able to integrate perspective constructions with site-specific imagery. In this chapter, pencil renderings were made by coordinating base drawings, mostly computer-generated perspective base drawings, with site photographs. A selection of modestly scaled interior and exterior perspective views is presented. In the case of interiors, trees and plants were added to the perspective construction. In the case of exteriors, constructed perspectives were added to existing site photographs.

A brief discussion of reflections and shade and shadow as they pertain to the depiction of buildings is also included in this chapter. Emphasis is on depicting the tonal values of shadows, not their actual construction.

## Perspective Constructions

Before an exterior or interior architectural drawing may be rendered in pencil tones, its design must first be constructed as a base line drawing.

129

This base line drawing serves as a kind of spatial template for the final rendering. It usually takes the form of a one- or two-point perspective.

In one-point perspective, rectangular rooms and buildings are viewed frontally. The one-point is constructed with a single vanishing point located at the center of the drawing's horizon line. In two-point perspective, on the other hand, rooms and buildings are viewed at oblique angles to the viewer's center of vision. Two-point perspectives include two vanishing points, one of which is almost always located out of the picture frame of the constructed view.

The two-point interior perspective construction in Figure 9–1 shows the basic skeletal line structure for the finished rendering in Figure 9–17. One of the two vanishing points for the perspective construction is visible in this drawing. It lies along the leading edge of the variable triangle. It also lies along the perspective construction's horizon line.

Perspective constructions for base drawings are either constructed mechanically by hand, as they have been for centuries, or they are generated on computer.

## Hand-Constructed Perspectives

A hand-constructed mechanical perspective is crafted in pencil from scratch, one tedious view at a time. Hand-drawn perspectives are either meticulously projected from plan and elevation views or constructed with the help of a perspective grid. Experienced delineators prefer to project perspectives because they obtain more control over the final viewing angle of their drawings. But constructing perspectives from scratch has its drawbacks even for experienced delineators. For example, there is the problem in two–point perspective of the faraway vanishing point. That is, in order to achieve a natural-looking view, one of the vanishing points for a two-point perspective construction must be located several feet away from the center of the drawing. Needless to say, it is sometimes difficult to find a table top large enough to physically locate faraway vanishing points.

Perspective grids, to their credit, are not only easy to learn how to use, they also do away with the problem of the faraway vanishing point. But we do pay a price for these conveniences. Perspective grids, the kind we purchase by the roll from an artist's supply store, are limited to the predetermined perspective frameworks and vanishing points that are furnished with the set. In addition, it is not uncommon to encounter multiple orientations of objects within the same perspective field. That is, the garage may be oriented at a skew angle to the house, in which case the perspective grid must be modified, or the skewed object must be located within the perspective framework point by point.

Regardless of whether the perspective is sketched on a blank sheet of paper or made with the aid of a perspective grid, the hand-drawn perspective will always be a useful graphic aid in the preliminary design phases of the rendering process. During preliminary studies, the experienced delineator can quickly sketch the look of a rendered scene with surprising accuracy. Not even the computer can muster the speed of the seasoned eye in capturing quick impressions of place.

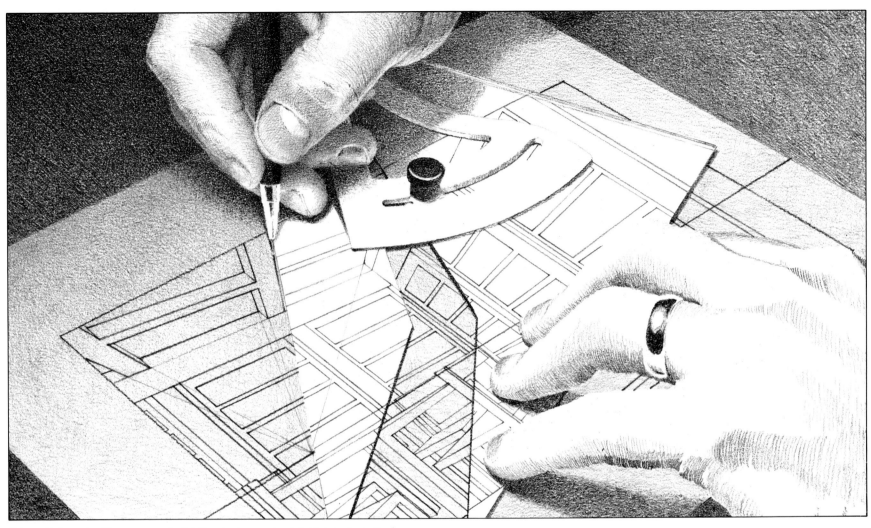

**Figure 9–1.** *An illustrator puts the finishing touches on a two-point interior perspective base drawing. Later, entourage will be added to this base drawing (Figure 9–15) in preparation for the final rendering (Figure 9–17).*

## Computer-Generated Perspectives

Computer-generated perspectives are rapidly replacing hand-drawn perspectives as the method of choice for mechanically constructing the base drawings of renderings (Figure 9–2). There are several good reasons for this. Equipment that a decade ago was as expensive to purchase as a new house can now be purchased for the price of a good stereo system. Minicomputers are also becoming increasingly user-friendly. The easier perspective construction programs can be learned by the novice in a single day.

The computer-generated perspective base drawings described in this chapter were constructed in three stages. First, plan and elevation views of objects in a scene were entered into the computer. Second, the vantage point for a desired perspective view was located in the computer's plan view. From this vantage point, the computer automatically generated a perspective view. Third, the computer program figured out overlap conditions in the perspective scene. That is, the computer automatically decided which surfaces in the perspective view were hidden and which were visible to the viewer. The view of the house on the computer screen in Figure 9–2 is an example of a computer perspective base drawing that was generated using these three steps.

Several modestly priced computer-perspective programs are able to perform these three functions well. In order to achieve realism beyond these three basic operations, however, computers must have the hardware and software to deal with far more calculations. These computations consume enormous amounts of processing time. Because of the computational time required to construct shade and shadow in the perspective view, for example, the shade and shadow algorithm is barely within the processing power of today's average computer owner.

There are computer programs today that can describe any conceivable photorealistic perspective effect. In order to simulate incident and reflective light on every surface in a perspective, for example, two types of computer programs are commonly used. One method is called ray tracing, the other radiosity. Ray tracing is view-dependent. Each time a new view of a scene is selected, a new set of calculations must be performed. Radiosity, on the other hand, is view independent. Once the surface values for a scene are calculated, the renderer can select any perspective viewpoint. Ray tracing programs may create photorealistic perspectives, but they consume lots of processing time. Radiosity algorithms simplify light intensity calculations. However, in exchange for this efficiency, they also tend to simplify the look of the rendered computer scene. Both algorithms are too slow to generate views of scenes depicting natural landscape features.

Perhaps by the year 2000, we may have inexpensive software programs that are simple to use and yet are capable of generating realistic scenes of enormous complexity. In the mean time, for the typical renderer, the computer makes sense only as a perspective construction tool. Pencil rendering continues to make sense as an alternative to advanced ray-tracing programs.

## Shade, Shadow, and Reflection

It is difficult to render perspectives without at least a few guidelines for establishing the tonal values of shade, shadow, and reflection. The working guidelines described on the following pages are discussed in greater detail by Steve Oles in his book, *Architectural Illustration: The Value Delineation Process*.

*Figure 9–2.* *Computer-constructed base perspectives for this book were constructed with a program called Architrion on a Macintosh Plus computer.*

By definition, there is a difference between shade and shadow. Surfaces in shade block sunlight from falling on surfaces in shadow. Shadows on horizontal surfaces are generally slightly darker than their shade counterparts on vertical surfaces (Figure 9–3). There is a reason for this: Sunlight bouncing off the horizontal ground plane slightly lightens the tonal value of shade on vertical surfaces. This effect may be modified by context.

Surfaces in sunlight vary slightly in tonal value depending upon their orientation to the angle of sunlight (Figure 9–4). The more a surface in sunlight is exposed to the direct, perpendicular rays of the sun, the lighter its value. As a corollary, parallel surfaces have constant tonal value.

Light reflected off adjacent surfaces creates subtle tonal gradations. In the depiction of the cube (Figure 9–5), note how the tonal value of the shaded face of the cube is slightly lighter at its base, due to the effects of reflected light.

Shadow edges gradually blur with distance from their source (Figure 9–6). Shadow intensity also diminishes with distance from its source. This effect, which is more noticeable for long shadows, may be confirmed by observing the shadows of trees and buildings.

The tonal value of a shadow on a dull surface is halfway between the tonal value of the surface in sunlight and pure black (Figure 9–7). This is a rule-of-thumb generalization that works effectively in most applications. Obviously, it would not make sense to simply add an absolute value of shadow to the intrinsic value of every surface case in shadow because no surface can be more than 100% black. In other words, a shadow that is 50% gray cast on a surface that is 60% gray yields a value of 80% gray, not 110%, which would be darker than pure black.

The rule for establishing the value of shadow on surfaces of different intrinsic values also applies to shade (Figure 9–8). A dull white surface in sunlight is depicted at 50 percent gray in shade. A 40 percent gray surface in sunlight is depicted in shade at halfway between 40 and 100 percent, or 70 percent gray.

Dark surfaces are more reflective than light ones (Figure 9–9). As a rule of thumb, reflected images are somewhat darker than objects reflected. There are circumstances that reverse this tendency. Reflected images may be lighter if they are either backlit or if they borrow reflected light from another source.

The view perpendicular to a surface is less reflective than the view of the same surface at an angle. For example, the view looking straight at a

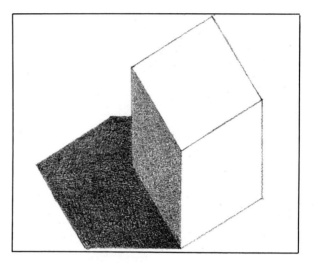

*Figure 9–3.    Shadows on horizontal surfaces are generally slightly darker than their shade counterparts on vertical surfaces.*

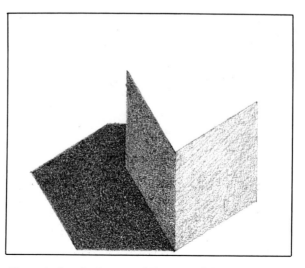

*Figure 9–4.    Surfaces in sunlight vary slightly in tonal value depending upon their orientation to the angle of sunlight.*

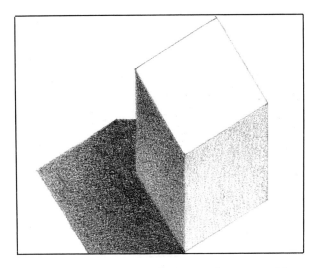

*Figure 9–5.* Light reflected off adjacent surfaces creates subtle tonal gradations.

*Figure 9–6.* Shadow edges gradually blur with increasing distance from their source.

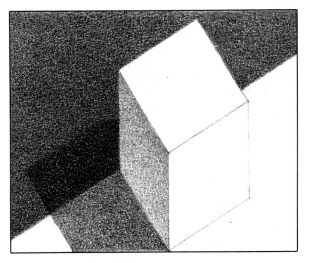

*Figure 9–7.* The tonal value of a shadow on a mat surface (the dark upper portion) is halfway between the tonal value of the surface in sunlight and pure black.

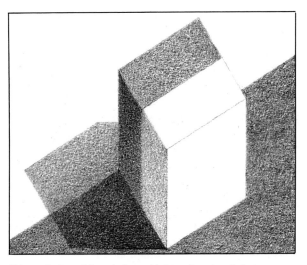

*Figure 9–8.* The rule for establishing the value of shadow on surfaces of different intrinsic values also applies to shade.

window is less reflective than the view of the same window as seen at an angle. The window behaves more like a mirror as it is viewed from increasingly oblique angles.

For double shadows, as a rule of thumb, treat the darker of two overlapping shadows as the intrinsic value of the surface receiving the double shadow, then add the value of the lighter shadow, using the halfway-to-black rule discussed earlier (Figure 9–10).

## Depicting Windows

One of the most complicated visual phenomena to depict with any degree of accuracy is the window. Its appearance is highly mutable and dependent on circumstances of context. On a sunny day, for example, the lighting level in the typical interior room of a house is roughly 1,000 times less than that of the outdoors. This pronounced difference in lighting level affects the appearance of windows on both sides of the glass. Here are a few working guidelines for rendering the window's appearance.

### Interior Windows

From the inside looking out, window openings look bright and light (Figure 9–11). Because of this, the primary tonal contrast in the rendering of interior spaces is generally between window pane and every other interior surface. Due to perceived simultaneous brightness contrast, this light/dark tonal contrast is especially pronounced for all interior features that silhouette against the window pane, such as the window's mullions and casings. We can observe this phenomena ourselves by simply squinting our eye as we look out an interior window. The resulting blur of shapes quickly reduces to a light/dark contrast between window and surrounding interior features. If windows are not made tonally lighter than their interior surroundings, they may appear more like pictures hanging on the wall than transparent openings to the brighter light outside.

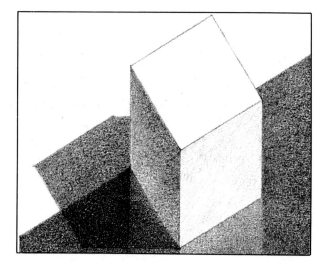

**Figure 9–9.** *Dark surfaces are more reflective than light ones.*

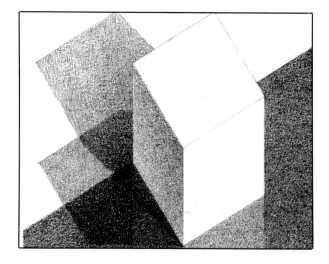

**Figure 9–10.** *For double shadows, as a rule of thumb, treat the darker of two overlapping shadows as the intrinsic value of the surface receiving the double shadow, then add the value of the lighter shadow, using the halfway-to-black rule discussed earlier.*

**Figure 9–11.** *Shade, shadow and reflection on interior surfaces.*

## Exterior Windows

In broad daylight, from the inside looking out, windows appear light and bright. These same windows appear dark when viewed from the outside, due to the extreme difference in interior and exterior lighting levels. Dark windows, like all other dark surfaces, have a tendency to behave as mirrors. For this reason, windows are more difficult to render from the exterior than the interior.

Every exterior window can first of all be visualized as if black in tone. This basic blackness is mitigated by three primary factors: (1) the angle at which the window is viewed; (2) the silhouetted views through the building of other windows; (3) features immediately behind the window such as pull shades and draperies.

## Viewing Angle

In broad daylight, the mirror quality of glass viewed from the outside is dependent upon the angle from which the glass is viewed. Generally, we may assume an exterior window viewed at a 45-degree angle is 90 percent reflective mirror and 10 percent transparent glass On the other hand, an exterior window viewed head-on is closer to 50 percent mirror and 50 percent glass.

The degree of reflectiveness is the degree to which the interior is not visible, except where interrupted by the reflection of a dark object.

First floor windows viewed head-on often appear black. This is because they reflect the dark masses of trees and buildings behind the viewer. Windows at higher levels reflect the sky and therefore appear lighter in appearance.

## Silhouette

Brightly lit shapes visible far behind the plane of the window glass can have a pronounced tonal influence on the basic black of the depicted window (Figure 9–12).

For example, if a window on the other side of the building is visible through the window opening that we are depicting, then the shape of the far window will appear as a light spot on an otherwise dark one. Other circumstances of bright lighting that may read through the basic blackness of our exterior window include lamps near the window, for example, a fluorescent light fixture in the ceiling. Direct sunlight streaming through a window opening and falling on an interior wall that is visible through the window may also interrupt the basically dark pattern of exterior windows.

## Backdrop

Dark surfaces are more reflective than light ones. Therefore, in daylight, the most important tonal feature of an exterior window is determined by what's immediately behind it. Does the window have curtains or draperies or blinds? If so, and assuming these curtains are white or off-white, the window will lose much of its black reflectiveness (Figure 9–13).

Are these window devices closed, open, or partially open? Illustrate curtains as white in the window. Indicate the shadow of mullions and sashes on the curtain or blind.

## Shadows on Transparent and Reflective Surfaces

Shadows do not fall upon reflective or transparent surfaces, which would rule out the possibility of casting a shadow of a tree, for example, on the glass of a window (Figure 9–14).

# Interior Perspective Views

The base drawings for the perspective renderings in this chapter were put together in two ways. The first involved adding bits and pieces of photographic imagery to the perspective construction; the second, placing or adding the perspective construction into a photographic depiction of the proposed context.

The method of adding fragments of entourage to base drawings is often used for interior perspectives, where the perspective construction itself serves as the spatial backdrop. Into the perspective setting the renderer adds the soft elements: the people, plants, and furniture that lend character to the space. There are several ways to add plant material to the base drawing of an interior perspective. One is to sketch these features into the perspective. Another is to overlay entourage cut from photographs or magazines to the perspective base drawing. Yet another is to perform the task completely on the computer screen, using scanned imagery.

A sunroom interior was constructed in perspective on computer (Figure 9–15). Table and chairs were positioned in the space by computer. This furniture was called up from a kind of electronic furniture showroom and pasted into the perspective view at an odd angle, not aligned with the grid lines of the room's perspective. This informal arrangement of table and chairs made the depicted space feel more natural, less formal. The plants were cut from pictures in old magazines. Because they were only lightly taped to the perspective construction, they could be reused later on. Wherever the plants appear to overlap constructed perspective features, like furniture, the perspective base drawing was cut with a knife and the plant imagery was slipped underneath. It was therefore possible to save the entourage for future renderings.

Several photocopies were made of the perspective with entourage and background. Some photocopies were used for diagrammatic tonal studies. They were sketched over quickly with a dull black pencil in order to establish shadow patterns, rendition of materials, and the tonal key of the final

*Figure 9–12.* *Windows visible through windows.*

*Figure* 9–13.  *Windows backed by curtains or pull shades.*

*Figure* 9–14.  *Windows that are both transparent and reflective.*

*Figure 9–15.* *A basic perspective construction is overlaid with pictures of plant material.*

rendering. Shadows of softer natural features were not constructed with absolute precision in the perspective.

After working out a satisfactory rough sketch of the rendering, shadows were included directly on a photocopied base rendering that included plant material. Tonal values were loosely assigned to various areas in the base drawing. This became the drawing that was eventually used as a base drawing in order to create the final rendered image of the sunroom.

Light from a hazy mid-afternoon sky pours into the sunroom through its windows and skylights (Figure 9–16). This drawing required approximately 24 hours to complete. It was rendered in several pencil layers. In the first of these layers, the challenging features were penciled in—I wanted to find out early if the plant material would look realistic (Figure 9–17). On a personal note, I prefer to tackle the most challenging features in the drawing first. I like to save the areas that I feel are easy to render for the very end. In other words, I prefer to find out right away if the drawing is going to succeed or fail. Other people, like my talented assistant, Don Aehl, prefer to layer renderings the other way around. They begin with the easy things and save the challenging parts of the drawing for last.

In the final version of the rendering, the foreground plant does not resemble its original appearance in the photocopy underlay (Figure 9–16). It was modified; made to feel more balanced and interesting by increasing the number of its limbs and leaves.

Sunlight pours into this space. The strong light/dark tonal contrast between the sunroom's many window frames and the bright outdoors enhances the room's sense of airy brightness. Frames around the windows were deliberately pushed toward a darker value to enhance this sense of illumination. Focus was established around the table and chair through the use of crisp black/white tonal contrasts. Light subtly streams across the plant in the background. The floor of the sunroom consists of a transparent layer of shadow over the intrinsic value of its surface pattern.

It is worth comparing this rendering with a previously rendered interior (Figure 9–11). In the case of the sunroom depicted here, for example, the plant material complements the architecture; whereas in Figure 9–11, only the cold architecture speaks. It is also worth noting the way that each rendering captures its overall sense of space. The rendering in Figure 9–17 lacks solid spatial definition because the room's third wall is noticeably absent. This is not the case in the room depicted in Figure 9–11.

***Figure** 9–16.* *Features in the Lake Park Lodge Sunroom rendering that were the most difficult to draw were penciled in first.*

**Figure 9–17.** *Lake Park Lodge Sunroom, interior view, rendered in 24 hours with Black no. 935 Berol Prismacolor pencil on Strathmore Alexis paper. Full-scale reproduction.*

*Figure 9–18.* *For exterior views, the building is added to the site photograph.*

# Exterior Perspective Views

Figure 9–18 depicts a building in the landscape which is made by adding the perspective of the building to the context and not the other way around. The usual procedure is to begin with a photograph of the existing context, then add or strip into the picture the hand-drawn or computer-generated perspective image.

Technically, adding perspective constructions to site photographs requires a basic understanding of certain perspective relationships. For this reason, it is a little more difficult to master than the method for generating interiors as described on the preceding pages. Above all else, it is important for the perspective construction to fit comfortably within the photograph of the context. Among other concerns, the constructed perspective must share a common horizon line with the subject matter in the photograph.

When working with computer-generated imagery, it is a good idea to know the rough measurements the existing site's basic plan layout (Figure 9–19). More specifically, at the time that we photograph the site, we should remember to plot the location of the station point (or spectator) in a measured plan view of the scene depicted. In order to do this, we simply have to pace off the rough plan dimensions of the existing site and note in this plan view where we are standing when we take the picture. It is also important to note in which direction we are facing as we take the photograph. The field of view of the camera lens should also be known. The lens on my camera, for example, has a 30-degree field of vision. When taking the photograph, an effort should be made to orient the camera lens so that it is level with the ground. A tripod is helpful in this matter. That way, both the photo and the perspective will be in the simpler framework of a two-point rendering. Vertical edges in two-point perspective remain vertical.

To fit the computer image into the photographic context, the horizon line should be located in both the computer image and the photograph. The plan coordinates that were duly noted at the time the site was photographed should be fed into the computer perspective's plan view. Lastly, the field of vision should be the same for both the computer perspective and the photograph. Thus, if the camera's lens has a 30-degree angle of vision, the computer perspective field of vision ought also to be 30 degrees.

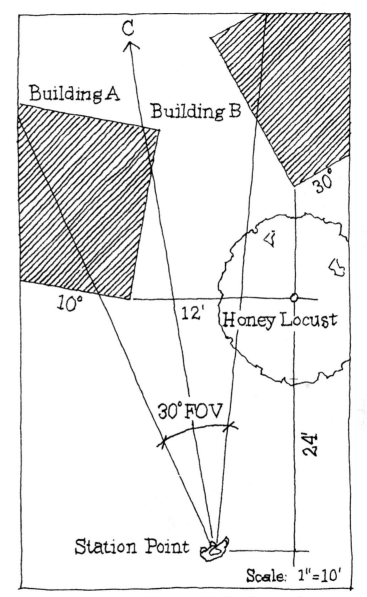

***Figure 9–19.*** *It is a good idea to record the plan dimensions of the site.*

If the computer image is sized properly, the resulting perspective should fit exactly into the site photograph.

## Adding Interest With Shadow Patterns

Scattered darks and lights animate wood surfaces loafing under the canopy of a shady tree (Figure 9–20). In order to render this scene, a computer-generated perspective of the featured building was layered into a photograph of the site. Preliminary sketches provided insight into the effectiveness of various methods for depicting shadow (Figures 9–21, 9–22).

The tall wooden fence in the foreground of Figure 9–20 directs the eye into the depicted space. Focus is located in the center of the picture, just toward the left and top of the sunroom.

We see no reflections of the surrounding landscape in the three sunroom doors because these doors are oriented frontal to our view. To relieve the monotony of the black interior that would otherwise be seen through the window panes in these doors, two doors include partly drawn pull shades. Note the shadow pattern of window mullions and tree branches on these shades. Note also the treatment of the five vertical window panes for the door on the far right. Again, to relieve the monotony of pure black windows, just a hint of light suggests the window opening on the opposite side of the house.

The shadow pattern in the midground, cast from left to right, is that of a tree unseen. The simple table and chair in midground are both washed in the shadow of this unseen tree. This furniture is literally broken into many pieces by the pattern of sunlight and shadow, yet our mind's eye fuses the many black and white pieces together in order to see table and chair. Observe the pattern of this same tree's shadow on the right foreground fence. Light holes are elliptical in shape, heavily foreshortened due to the raking angle of the wall. The tree's shadows also serve to link the house to the ground plane.

Trees in the background are rendered with a broader, less detailed line technique than features in the foreground and midground. The silhouette of sunporch against house is stronger than the silhouette between house and background trees.

*Figure 9–20.* Lake Park Lodge with sunroom and patio, rendered in 16 hours with Black Berol Prismacolor no. 935 on Strathmore Alexis paper. Full-scale reproduction.

*Figure 9–21.*   *Lake Park Lodge with sunroom and patio: Preliminary pencil study.*

*Figure 9–22.*   *Lake Park Lodge with sunroom and patio: Preliminary tonal study.*

## Tonal Mood

The site for the Hartford Avenue Public Lounge was a flat plot of land surrounded by trees and buildings (Figure 9–23). In order to depict the proposed design, a computer perspective of the lounge was sized and oriented to fit into a photograph of the existing site. This collage image became the base drawing for the final rendering.

In terms of composition, a large existing foreground tree frames the view of the darkly moody pictorial space. The viewer's eye is meant to focus on the light-filled double-height windows of the lounge. Glowing strings of light weave their way through the branches of the tree in the midground.

The drawing was rendered in layers. With each successive layer of pencil strokes, the image became darker and mossier. Early versions of the drawing were considerably lighter in value (Figure 9–24). The tonal study for the final drawing bears a remarkable resemblance to the final depiction (Figure 9–25). This tonal study was done with black pencil on photocopies of the computer perspective taped to the site photograph.

*Figure 9–23.* Hartford Avenue Public Lounge, rendered in 20 hours with Black Berol Prismacolor no. 935 on Strathmore Alexis paper. Full-scale reproduction.

**Figure 9–24.** *Hartford Avenue Public Lounge, preliminary version.*

**Figure 9–25.** *Photocopied enlargement of site photo with computer-generated perspective overlay.*

*Figure 9–26.* House on Fredrick Avenue, rendered in 20 hours with Black Berol Prismacolor no. 935 on Strathmore Alexis paper. Full-scale reproduction.

## Interest Through Focus and Shadow

The site for this modest home was a vacant lot located in the midst of an otherwise continuous row of 1920s Victorian houses. The rendered scene portraying this little home in context was traced from a site photograph overlaid with a computer-generated perspective image of the house (Figure 9–26). Pencil was applied to the rendering in several layers. For the sake of comparison, an earlier version of the finished rendering is included (Figure 9–27).

The final rendering has a forced focus. The purest whites are reserved only for the brightest highlights—around the house's front door. Everything else has tone. Shadows were added to create visual interest. The otherwise blank house facade is animated with the shadow of foreground trees. Note that this shadow pattern clarifies rather than obscures the definition of molded form on the surface of the house's facade.

*Figure 9–27.   House on Fredrick Avenue, early version. The tone has not yet been completely built up.*

# Aerial Perspective

The late afternoon light is hazy and brilliant. The drafting pavilion, a building in miniature, huddles close to the sidewalk on this quiet street in Milwaukee (Figure 9–28).

A perspective image of the pavilion was generated on computer, then fit into a photograph of the existing site (Figure 9–29). The eye level for the computer perspective was made to coincide with the eye level of the person who took the picture: 5' 6". Other site measurements, duly recorded at the time that the picture was taken, were fed as coordinates into the computer perspective.

The whole of the rendered space is organized hierarchically, in aerial perspective. Depth of field filters out contrasts. The pavilion in the foreground has the greatest detail; the trees and car in the background have the least contrast and definition.

Other miscellaneous rhetorical effects were incorporated into the rendering. For example, on the shady side of the pavilion, the grout lines separating the stone veneer panels of the pavilion's facade are depicted in white. These same lines reverse to black as they turn round the corner to the front facade. The connection between the grass ground plane and the drafting pavilion was also carefully considered. The base of the pavilion is rendered with irregular green tufts of grass sprouting all around. The lawn around the pavilion is depicted in closely spaced horizontal streaks, suggesting the foreshortening of tree shadows.

The sidewalk is sunny. The front facade of the pavilion, bathed in late afternoon light, is visually prominent in the rendering because it silhouettes against the shady side of the building just behind it. The winter tree in the right foreground of the rendering is rendered as if in intense light—black for shadow, white for surfaces in sunlight—in order to bring the tree forward in the space. Rendering the tree in both black and white gave it greater visual prominence than if it had been rendered in silhouette, i.e., completely black. In order to enhance the feeling of sunlight beating down on the ground, the effect of reflected light is captured in the subtly graduated shadowed wall of the building. The effects of sunlight were also considered in the building's details. The little square window in the gable of the pavilion is rendered like the windows of the adjacent building. In each case, the whole shape of the window is only hinted at. Certain key lines are omitted from each depicted window. This creates the effect of sunlight so bright that it bleaches out certain details. Finally, the rendering as a whole was deliberately pushed toward figure/ground, that is, it was decided beforehand to use mostly harsh black and white tones. Because of this, the viewer should be able to feel the heat of the sun blazing on the front facades of the buildings.

*Figure 9–28.* *Photocopied enlargement of site photo with computer-generated perspective overlay.*

*Figure 9–29.* *Marietta Street Drafting Pavilion, rendered in 16 hours with Black Berol Prismacolor no. 935 on Strathmore Alexis paper. Full-scale reproduction.*

# Depth of Field

Cottage, garage, and distant pergola were constructed on computer. A properly oriented and sized computer perspective of these architectural elements was pasted into a site photograph. The composite image of site photograph and computer image were photocopied. This became the base drawing for the final pencil rendering (Figure 9–30).

The rendering is composed as a kind of set piece. Through choice of vantage point, movement of the eye into the depths of this rendering proceeds in a zigzag pattern. The eye enters the picture from the right, bounces off the raking foreground plane of the garage, then deflects off the stand of trees to the right. The eye then proceeds to the center of the picture, where it dwells in the midground of the pictorial space, on the front porch of the little cottage. The tonal emphasis of the drawing is focused on the cottage's porch.

In the background of the drawing, beyond the forced silhouette of the cottage, is an irregular horizontal band of low tonal contrast that is meant to suggest distant features of the landscape.

The rendering as a whole is set up so as to embrace the viewer. The central feature of the drawing, the little cottage, is comfortably nestled between two near and prominent foreground features. These foreground elements play off one another. The stand of trees is intricate, flat and frontal, whereas the garage is simple, volumetric, and deep.

The garage, trees, and cottage are tonally linked together through the emphasis given to their collective silhouette against the bright, white sky. This forced silhouette tonally groups features in the foreground and midground together, setting them off from the distant horizontal band in the background. Tonal weight is toward the bottom of the composition.

*Figure 9–30.* *Garage and Cottage on Chantilly Lane, rendered in 12 hours with Black Berol Prismacolor no. 935 on Strathmore Alexis paper. Full-scale reproduction.*

# Bibliography

Adams, William, *The French Garden*, New York: George Braziller, 1979.

Arnheim, Rudolf, *Visual Thinking*, Berkeley: University of California Press, 1969.

Arnheim, Rudolf, *The Power of the Center*, Berkeley: University of California Press, 1982.

Ching, Frank, *Architectural Graphics*, 2d ed., New York: Van Nostrand Reinhold, 1985.

Clifford, Derek, *A History of Garden Design*, New York, Praeger, 1963.

Cottin, Lin, *All About Landscaping*, San Francisco: Ortho Books, 1980.

Cullen, Gordon, *The Concise Townscape*, New York: Van Nostrand Reinhold, 1961.

Fisher, Thomas, "Presenting Ideas," *Progressive Architecture*, pp. 84–93, June 1989.

Gernsheim, Helmut and Alison, *L. J. M. Daguerre*, Cleveland: World Publishing Company, 1956.

Gibson, James J., *The Perception of the Visual World*, Boston: Houghton Mifflin, 1950.

Gilpin, William, *Three Essays on Picturesque Beauty*, 2d ed., London: printed for R. Blamire, 1794.

Goldwater, Robert and Marcos Treves, *Artists on Art*, New York: Pantheon Books, 1945.

Gothein, Marie, *A History of Garden Art*, edited by Walter P. Wright. Translated from the German by Mrs. Archer-Hind, New York: Hacker Art Books, 1966.

Guptill, Arthur L., *Rendering in Pen and Ink*, rpt., New York: Watson-Guptill Publications, 1976.

Guptill, Arthur L., *Rendering in Pencil*, rpt., edited by Susan E. Meyer, New York: Watson-Guptill Publications, 1977.

Hiss, Tony, *The Experience of Place*, New York: Knopf, 1990.

Jellicoe, Geoffrey and Susan, *The Landscape of Man*, New York: Van Nostrand Reinhold, 1975.

McGinty, Tim, *Drawing Skills in Architecture*, Dubuque, Iowa: Kendall/Hunt Publishing Company, 1976.

Newton, Norman, *Design on the Land: The Development of Landscape Architecture*, Cambridge, Mass.: Belknap Press of the Harvard University Press, 1971.

Oles, Paul Stevenson, *Architectural Illustration: The Value Delineation Process*, New York: Van Nostrand Reinhold, 1979.

Orgel, Stephen and Roy Strong, *Inigo Jones: The Theater of the Stuart Court, Volume Two*, London: Sotheby Parke Bernet; Berkeley and Los Angeles: University of California Press, 1973.

Pyne, J.B., "The Nomenclature of Pictorial Art," (London) *Art-Union*, 6 (1844):42.

Ruskin, John, *The Elements of Drawing*, London 1857: rpt., New York: Dover Publications, 1971.

Scholz, Janos, *Baroque and Romantic Stage Design*, New York: E. P. Dutton, 1962.

Serlio, Sebastiano, *The Five Books of Architecture, An Unabridged Reprint of the English Edition of 1611*, New York: Dover Publications, 1982. Originally published: *The first {-fift} booke of architecture*. London: Printed for R. Peake, 1611.

Shepard, Geoffrey and Susan Jellicoe, *Italian Gardens of the Renaissance*, Library ed. London: Tiranti, 1966.

Weber, Ernst A., *Vision, Composition and Photography*, New York: De Gruyter, 1980.

Wilmerding, John, *American Light*, Princeton: Princeton University Press, 1989.

Zion, Robert L., *Trees for Architecture and the Landscape*, New York: Van Nostrand Reinhold, 1968.

# Index